RIG 'EM

RIG 'EM

A Case Study of Leadership Failure in the Tenure and Promotion Process

Leonard Bright

Copyright © 2025 Leonard Bright

All rights reserved. No part of this publication may be produced, distributed, or transmitted in any form or by any means, including photocopying, recording, or other electronic or mechanical methods, without permission of the publisher, except with brief quotations embodied in critical reviews and certain other non-commercial uses permitted by copyright law.

ISBN: 979-8-9933874-0-6 (Electronic Book)
ISBN: 979-8-9933874-1-3 (Paperback)
ISBN: 979-8-9933874-2-0 (Hardback)

Library of Congress Control Number: (Requested)

The events described in this book are based on the author's interpretation of real events. Some characters involved have been fictionalized by the author in terms of their names and identifying details. The perspectives and opinions expressed are solely the author's and do not represent any individual, institution, or organization mentioned in the book. The information presented in this book should not be interpreted as legal advice on any matter, but only for academic research, informational, and/or educational purposes.

Book Cover and Design by Fun Graphics.

The Bright Media Couple LLC
2130 Harvey Mitchell Pkwy S #10553
College Station, TX 77842

Drleonardbright.com

DEDICATION

Foremost, to my wife, Christina I love you. We stood together through it all.

I would like to thank the reviewers for offering vital revisions to an early version of this manuscript.

To all the individuals who provided me with their advice and counsel before and during my academic journey, I extend my deepest gratitude.

CONTENTS

Dramatis Personae ix

Preface xi

Prologue 1

Chapter 1: The Situation 15

Chapter 2: The Beginning 33

Chapter 3: The Contamination 45

Chapter 4: Cooking the Books 69

Chapter 5: The Defense 81

Chapter 6: The New Beginning 105

Epilogue 119

Notes 139

References 141

Appendixes 153

Index 253

DRAMATIS PERSONAE

Key Acronyms

AAUP	American Association of University Professors
CPC	College Promotion Committee
DOF	Dean of Faculties
DPC	Department Promotion Committee
EEOC	Equal Employment Opportunity Commission
OREC	Office of Risk, Ethics, & Compliance
UGC	University Grievance Committee

Key Characters

Dr. Katherine Banks	3rd university president
Christina Bright	Dr. Bright's wife & part-time instructor
Ryan Crocker	1st college dean
Professor Gerber	promotion candidate #2
Dr. Susan G. Green	2nd department head
Dr. Hopkins	1st department head
Dr. Johnson	2nd *interim* department head
Dr. Ramsdel	DPC chair & 1st *interim* department head
Professor Vaughn	promotion candidate #1
Mark Welsh	2nd college dean & 4th university president
Dr. Michael Young	2nd university president

PREFACE

As you embark on this journey through the pages of this book, I want to extend my heartfelt gratitude for your interest and time. This work of nonfiction is a documented reflection of my personal experiences and observations within the academic workplace, spanning over two decades. I hope that by sharing my story, I can provide insight, knowledge, and perhaps a sense of support to those who may navigate similar challenges.

The core events described are based on a true story. Besides my personnel files, other documents, reports, emails, interview transcripts, etc. addressed in this book are public information received through the Equal Employment Opportunity Commission (EEOC), open records requests, and legal proceedings in Texas. Some names and identifying details have been changed to protect privacy. The perspectives and opinions expressed are solely mine and do not represent any individual, institution, or organization mentioned in the book. This book does not provide legal advice on any matter. Before acting on any information or material in this book, seek professional legal counsel.

My goal is to shed light on the intricacies and often unspoken realities of the tenure and promotion process and to highlight the importance of effective leadership oversight. Through this narrative, I aim to inspire positive changes and encourage constructive dialogue about the issues that persist in academic workplaces. In 2023, I even created a YouTube channel called *"The Bright Professor"* that extends the goals of this book.

Thank you for joining me on this journey. I trust you will find the content both thought-provoking and enlightening.

PROLOGUE

Rig 'em: A colloquial term that refers to something that has been manipulated or unfairly influenced to produce a desired outcome, often to the disadvantage of others.[1]

I applied for a promotion to the rank of full professor, and I alleged my colleagues rigged the process against me. When I started my academic career twenty years ago, I would not have imagined I would make such a statement, since I was sure I knew the path to success. As a young assistant professor, fresh out of graduate school, I hit the ground running. I believed my future would include collegiality and collaboration. I believed I would receive invitations to join research partnerships, that colleagues would support me, and that my field would value my contributions. Over the years, I worked diligently, and for the most part, I enjoyed it. However, I did this despite the hostility I experienced in the academic work culture that sought to drive me out of the profession.

Before I even became a college professor, I already knew that the tenure and promotion process at some universities was problematic. As college students, my wife Christina and I both held part-time jobs on campus. Unbeknownst to me, Christina's job would give critical insight that would help me many years later as a college professor. My wife's job required her to transcribe the meeting notes for senior administrators. She learned about the deceitful tactics that some department faculty members had used to help or injure their own colleagues during their tenure and promotion process. This troubled her, and she wanted to talk about it when she got home. Christina observed that some university administrators corrected improper behavior, while others did not. From her recollection, a vocal graduate school dean would often remind colleagues that inappropriate behavior in one part of the university reflected poorly on the entire institution.

Today, I can confirm from personal experience that the problems I learned over 20 years ago are still alive in many academic workplaces. These issues await faculty members who, for reasons unrelated to performance, find themselves on the *"not supported"* roster. Faculty members can spend hundreds of thousands of dollars on their education and contribute years of grinding hard work developing their careers. You can easily imagine the financial and emotional burden of being denied tenure or promotion without an obvious reason, especially when it contradicts earlier evaluations or when compared to how other, more favored colleagues were treated.

My Academic Career

My first tenure-track position was at the University of South Alabama, which was a regional teaching university. After two years, I left there for a tenure-track assistant professor position at the University of Louisville (UofL). I was the first black faculty member ever hired into my department, and on my very first day, the resentment that I felt from my colleagues was palpable. Some of the faculty believed that they were forced to hire me by the university to add a black faculty member in the department. My department immediately used my annual, tenure, and promotion review processes as their chief weapons against me in an ongoing battle with the university, drafting me onto the front-lines.

Amazingly, this situation helped me to hone my skills in academic warfare. My colleagues learned quickly that I was no pushover. I was more than capable of fighting for myself against their mistreatment and misleading assessments of my performance. One of the most important and impactful characteristics of UofL that helped me was its annual and tenure review rebuttal processes. I used these processes to rebut their erroneous assessments vigorously. Despite my high performance, my struggle culminated with the department's unsurprising vote to deny my tenure and promotion to associate professor after five years of harassment and hostility.

In the end, I won the war at UofL. Thankfully, my college dean, provost, and university president had the courage to push against my department's resistance and grant me the tenure and promotion that I had earned. Early in the promotion process, I had to make the tough decision to file an EEOC complaint to address the situation. At one point, I was concerned that my decision to call in the EEOC would paint me as disloyal and difficult and thus damage my academic career in the future. These worries are no longer mine. I understood I faced only two options: succumb to a department determined to end my career within the university or employ every resource available to counterattack. Having chosen the latter choice, I have no regrets.

When a hostile workplace targets an employee, it is to their advantage to convince the targeted employee to make it easy, while dangling the false hope that the situation may change if they remain silent and compliant. Silence and conformity will not change the bad intentions of a hostile workplace. Some faculty members at UofL were unwavering in their efforts to end my academic career. If I had remained silent, made it easy, and refused to fight back, they would have succeeded. Even more, it was important to me that I fight back on my behalf, even if the results were likely to be unfavorable. Why should I expect help from others if I am unwilling to fight for myself first? If my career ended, I would rather it ended with me fighting on my feet.

Subsequently, while under tenure and promotion review at UofL, I went on the job market and applied for a tenured associate professor position at Texas A&M University's Bush School of Government and Public Service in College Station, Texas. Later, I discovered that controversy also filled the circumstances of my hiring at Texas A&M. Although they offered me the associate professor position, I learned from the department head (Dr. Hopkins) that most of the tenured faculty members voted against offering me tenure. I feared the Bush School faculty knew about my EEOC complaint and were trying to sabotage my job offer. Even though I had no hard proof that communications were going on between UofL and Texas A&M faculty, I had circumstantial evidence.

In fact, I had received multiple emails from my department chair at UofL informing me he had learned of my application to the Bush School and demanding that I confirm my plans to leave the university. I ignored his demands since I had not yet accepted any job offers. Since I had not earned tenure and was still in the tenure review process at UofL, I was required to undergo the entire tenure review process at Texas A&M. It took courageous leadership from the Bush School's dean, former U.S. Ambassador Ryan Crocker, who rejected the faculty's recommendations. They offered me the job with tenure at the associate professor rank. I accepted Texas A&M's offer, and as one can imagine, this did not go over well with some of the senior faculty members I would work alongside in the coming years. Once again, I entered an academic workplace with growing resentment and disdain toward me. The academic performance management system is fraught with complexities and inconsistencies that demand closer scrutiny.

Academic Performance Management

Most would agree that fairness and consistency are essential principles in any workplace. The theory of human resource management (HRM) has significantly contributed to upholding these principles, particularly in performance management. Performance management aims to improve employee output. It aligns output with clear organizational goals. This ensures fair treatment. Employees with similar achievements are treated alike. Those with different achievements are treated differently.

Universities use many performance management techniques to evaluate college professors. These techniques include multifaceted goals, multistage evaluation processes, peer feedback, and student input. Using these techniques gives the outward appearance of fair, thorough, and careful performance management practices. Yet, these features offer little protection from the influences of subjective, preferential, and poor treatment in academic departments for at least three reasons.

Clear Goals Are Rare in Academia

First, clear performance goals are rare in most academic departments, especially in tenure and/or promotion decisions. This is an intentional feature of the academic environment. Scholarly achievement differs from widget production, where clear outcomes are much easier to create and agree on. For instance, in a company that manufactures running shoes, there is likely little debate over what constitutes a running shoe or how many pairs must be sold to generate revenue. Conversely, regarding academic performance goals, faculty members are prone to disagree with the most basic aspects. College professors, for instance, must produce impactful research in their areas of expertise. However, many academic departments lack a universal, objective, consistent, and agreed-upon method to determine when faculty members have achieved this. As a result, performance management decisions in academic departments are subjectively determined. This opens the door to decisions being influenced by non-performance-based considerations and biases. When this happens, the true reasons for biased decisions are not recorded in meeting minutes, rarely discussed aloud, and/or justified in the haze of subjective performance goals. Some faculty members may feel that their only options are to help the team, ignore the situation, or risk becoming targets.

The Freedom to Decide is Protected

Second, the freedom to define subjective performance goals in the tenure and promotion process on a case-by-case basis is a fiercely protected feature of the academic culture and performance management system. There is a firm belief in academia that the faculty should determine who works alongside them, including who gets tenured and promoted in the faculty ranks. One of the nation's oldest and most prestigious faculty associations, the American Association of University Professors (AAUP) codified such expectations. Founded in 1915, the AAUP's primary mission is to advance academic freedom and shared governance. In October 1966, the association published its *Statement on Government of Colleges and Universities* [2] where they took the following positions regarding the academic performance management process:

> *The role of the faculty is to have primary responsibility for such fundamental areas as faculty status which includes appointments, reappointments, decisions not to reappoint, promotions, the granting of tenure, and dismissal.*
>
> *Faculty have special training and knowledge that make them distinctly qualified to exercise decision-making authority in their areas of expertise. And they are best qualified to judge the competence and effectiveness of fellow faculty members.*
>
> *Even though the president and board may possess final authority, they should routinely concur with faculty recommendations made in*

> *areas of faculty responsibility and should reject faculty decisions in those areas only in rare instances and for compelling reasons which should be stated in detail. In short, when it comes to academic matters, a faculty decision should normally be the final decision.*

The AAUP's stance on faculty governance has profoundly shaped the academic workplace. It promoted the principle that faculty should be able to make the most important decisions in academic performance management. However, the AAUP's *"compelling reasons"* clause leaves some room to question at the very least faculty decisions that are biased, preferential, and inconsistent. Yet, even when clear problems occur in the performance management process, there are some who cannot even acknowledge the possibility that rare *"compelling"* problems may be the issue. There are some who believe that faculty decisions can never be wrong in the end. University administration and lawyers also promote this view when it is in their interest to do so, to shield themselves from outside accountability. When Texas A&M administrators faced clear and compelling evidence to scrutinize the faculty's decision in my case, they argued that the evidence should not be considered, based on *"academic determination."*

Academia is a Collective

Third, the tenure and promotion process gives faculty the ability to ensure the success of colleagues they support and to work toward the failure of colleagues they do not support. Human resource management theory defines performance management at the level of the individual. It assumes that the performance outcomes of one employee do not directly influence those of another employee. Even when employees work in teams, some approaches will delimit and assess each employee's effort separately. This view does not match academic workplace realities. Most academic departments operate collectively. Often when the department supports a faculty member, it will partner with them on research projects, help them meet the *"promotion standards,"* and even ignore those standards if that becomes necessary to get their preferred candidate over the line.

For example, single-authored publications were the gold standard in academia as they showed a scholar's ability to produce research independently. However, the use of publication teams has become increasingly common and valuable.[3] This is a situation where scholars team up to produce published research. Using this strategy, a single publication can list multiple authors, who can all claim credit and responsibility for the lion's share of the work at their respective institutions. There is little doubt that the energy it takes to produce research using a team of scholars is less than it would take for scholars who produce the same published works independently. Teams are also significantly more effective at producing multiple publications quickly. However, tenure and promotion reviews seldom fully acknowledge these facts, especially when unsupported faculty are intentionally excluded from research teams but still are expected to do the same amount of work independently. Hence, the actual performance and success of some professors were not solely their own, but a sign of the level of support they enjoyed. Those who have the support of their colleagues often prosper, while those who do not will have a much harder road to success.

The reality of academic performance management is often at odds with the ideals of fairness and transparency. While my experience highlights the unique challenges and obstacles encountered in pursuit of advancement, it is far from an isolated case. Indeed, a growing body of research has explored the broader patterns and systemic issues that shape promotion practices across academia.

Research on the Full Professor Rank

Seven years after being hired at Texas A&M as a tenured associate professor, I applied for promotion to the full professor rank. The full professor rank is one of the highest achievements in the academy. Yet, research on the experiences of faculty members seeking promotion to this level is elusive. Many studies focus on assistant professors seeking tenure and promotion. Few studies explore the experiences of faculty seeking the rank of full professor. Several factors make it difficult to apply the experiences of faculty seeking tenure and promotion to the experiences of faculty seeking the rank of full professor.

For starters, most universities mandate that assistant professors be reviewed for tenure after a set period, but this is not the case for those aiming to be full professors. After earning tenure and being promoted to associate professor, there is no obligation to pursue the full professor rank. Next, a negative decision on promotion to full professor rarely leads to job loss, unlike the situation for assistant professors seeking tenure. Finally, while it is believed that the standards for full professor promotion are much higher than for associate professor, this has not been definitively proven. Existing research on the experiences of those seeking full professor rank reveals two key findings.

Ambiguous Performance Goals

First, ambiguity shrouds the standards for promotion. While assistant professors seeking tenure routinely complain about this problem, the confusion level is significantly more profound among associate professors. For example, a group of faculty members who were denied full promotion or discouraged from applying described their experiences as *dumbfounding*.[4] This research shows that many associate professors who are interested in pursuing further advancement must interpret encrypted clues from their senior colleagues. The lack of clear performance benchmarks has convinced many that the full professor rank is out of their reach.[5]

Gender and Racial Disparities

Second, the research on the full promotion process shows that gender and racial disparities are prevalent. According to the 2022 National Center for Educational Statistics, only 19% of full professors were nonwhite in the United States. Asian professors made up the largest minority group among full professors at 12%, compared to Black professors, who made up only 4% of these positions.[6] So, not only are Black faculty members significantly less likely to be hired and tenured, but they are also significantly less likely to be promoted to the rank of full professor.[7]

There is also evidence that gender is a major determinant of one's promotability, even though female faculty members, especially white females, have made great gains over the years. When compared to their male counterparts, women spend more time at the rank of associate professor, are more likely to be discouraged from applying for promotion and are significantly less likely to achieve full promotion when they apply. Although some may believe that the achievements of women and faculty members of color make them less competitive than their white male counterparts, research has shown racial and gender disparities, even when considering research productivity.[8] For example, since my arrival at the Bush School, the only faculty who were denied tenure and/or promotion were three women and a black male (me).

The research shows that ambiguity in the performance standards for promotion to full professor negatively impacts faculty. Many faculty members find these expectations difficult to understand, and this issue is compounded by substantial gender and racial disparities in achieving the rank. These challenges underscore the need for clearer benchmarks, more equitable advancement processes, and a better understanding of promotion procedures within academia. This book will expand upon these findings, drawing on my personal experiences with the promotion process at Texas A&M.

The Call That Started It All

Texas A&M's decision to deny my first application for promotion to the full professor rank influenced my decision to write this book. I received a phone call from the new department head informing me that a three-person department committee had voted unanimously against my application for promotion. She stated their reasons centered on their opinion that my research was not impactful in my field. She made multiple other statements, and they confirmed my suspicion that they had treated me differently from other colleagues recently promoted. I believed that their decision had nothing to do with my actual performance, and I wanted to get to the bottom of it. So, just like my decision at UofL, I initiated an EEOC investigation. This investigation yielded valuable information and documents that this case study will explore.

Book Purpose

This book is an illustrative research case study of my experiences in the promotion process at Texas A&M University. Case studies are excellent for addressing how, what, and why inquiries within actual situations. This book will build on these benefits and will provide multiple observation points using my own records and affiliated documents. This includes my complete promotion dossier, letters from external reviewers, and all available deliberation memos. Also included are relevant emails, analyses, and reports from faculty, committees, and administrators. I lightly edited most of the documents for clarity. However, I took great care to ensure that the original intent of these documents remained intact. Within each chapter's narrative, I have incorporated these records, which also exist in their entirety within this book's appendices. They capture those who evaluated my work in their own words, as well as the written responses

I had to them. I encourage readers to read it all, form their own opinions and reach their own conclusions. As far as I am aware, there is no comparable contribution that exists within libraries or academic writing.

Book Goals

In addition, this book accomplishes several goals. First, it seeks to demystify academic performance management. I have served as a member of the academy for two decades. This has been both a privilege and an honor. It is a fulfilling career, despite the immense challenges. I want to arm those pursuing academic careers with a realistic understanding of the challenges they may face and the tools to fight for fairness. This book provides information that I wish I had when I entered the academy as a young tenure-track faculty member years ago. It may have helped me anticipate the issues that I faced and provided options for how to address them.

Second, as I explained, there is a dearth of research on the full promotion process. I want to contribute my case to the limited body of research. The case material will give researchers and human resource professionals a firsthand opportunity to study my case in detail. Additionally, I hope that my example encourages others who have experienced similar situations to contribute their own experiences to the field.

Third, this case study demonstrated the importance of effective academic leadership. There are genuine problems that exist in academic performance management that require effective, courageous leadership. When problems occur, administrators are among the first individuals called upon. However, some administrators' priorities are not always to resolve these concerns but to protect their organizations against external and internal threats. Often, this has led some leaders to bind together and work against those who are voicing their concerns about poor treatment. Professors who lack awareness may find this discouraging. My book will show what happened when I raised important issues and concerns regarding the performance management processes I underwent. It will highlight the myriad strategies used, and the arguments made by university leaders to resist efforts to address the problems I uncovered. This book details what can happen when administrators fail to guard the basic principles of accountability, consistency, and fairness.

Fourth, I want to encourage those who are engaged in their own fights against unfair treatment to fight on. The EEOC has received over one million employment discrimination complaints since 2010. Yet, less than two percent of EEOC investigations have found evidence that supports allegations of discrimination.[9] Discrimination allegations have not fared well in courts either. The complexity and ambiguity of the academic environment have made courts hesitant about substituting their judgements for those made by such distinguished faculty. Many universities have taken full advantage of this situation. Even when qualifiable evidence of wrongdoing is available, some institutions will do their best to restrict access to it. This can even include conducting faulty investigations to discourage complainants. When this occurs, the EEOC and similar state-level agencies are indispensable. My EEOC representative worked hard as an impartial investigator. The information that I recommended she gather helped me pinpoint alleged instances of discrimination and retaliation. Their investigation gave me the critical records that helped me obtain proof of what had been done. This book contains many of these documents. I hope readers who are in similar or even worse situations know their rights and have the courage to act on them.

Last, my experience should not be overgeneralized. They may not apply to every individual, department, college, or university. I am sure that there are departments and faculty members who have proactively worked hard to overcome the worst tendencies of the academic workplace, and even human nature. Some may have even jeopardized their own career advancements and professional relationships to help solve them. These sacrifices earn my respect, though further effort remains.

Book Outline

This book has several chapters. The first chapter describes the moment I learned of the recommendation against my promotion application and what I did about it. In Chapter 2, readers will revisit the start of the story, where the circumstances that surrounded my hiring will be examined. Chapter 3 will closely scrutinize the solicitation of the external reviewers. Chapter 4 explores how the department and college faculty committees used the external reviewer letters to justify their conclusions. The chapter also includes a comparative analysis of my research accomplishments and those of two other faculty promoted in the department. Chapters 5 and 6 describe the actions of university officials to divert attention from my claims. The chapters will also describe their efforts to conceal the results of internal investigations, which revealed what I believed were inconsistencies in my promotion process. The epilogue will summarize the lessons learned from this case and offer words of advice to faculty members and university leaders.

CHAPTER 1:

The Situation

Something had gone wrong in my promotion process. My first update arrived from our new department head, Dr. Susan G. Green. I was away for the holidays when she called to inform me that a three-member department promotion committee (DPC) had voted against my application, and that four of the six external reviewers[10] were not supportive. The DPC was responsible for reviewing my application and issuing its recommendation to the department head. Three days later, I penned the following message to the college dean, retired United States General Mark Welsh, summarizing the conversation and my concerns about the encounter. Below is an abridged summary of my message (see Appendix A for the full text).

Email from Dr. Bright to Dean Welsh about Dr. Green

Dean Welsh,

Dr. Green gave me an update on the status of my application for promotion to full professor. She indicated that a three-member faculty committee voted against my application. Based on my conversation with her, it is clear that she is unable and unwilling to advocate for my record. Obviously, I have not worked with her as department head given that she has been in the position for one semester. I must take this drastic step to advocate for what I have accomplished.

More arduous research standards are being applied to my case that have not been applied to other similarly situated faculty members. She stated that my scholarly impact was more consistent with the standards for promotion to associate professor rather than to full professor. This insult suggests that I should not have been hired as a tenured associate professor seven years ago when I had fewer accomplishments.

Dr. Green asked me to withdraw my application because I will lack the support (presumably) from you and/or other higher-level decision makers, even if she chooses to "weakly support" my application. When I refused, she stated that my decision "was a mistake." I understood this to be a threat that I would never be promoted if I moved forward. I have no intention of withdrawing my application and will see this all the way to the end.

It is not lost on me that I am the only tenured or tenure-track African American faculty at the entire Bush School. I am taking the unusual step of asking you to look past the few faculty attempts to dismiss my great overall performance record, as Dr. Green intends to do.

I am free to meet with you regarding these concerns at any time you are available. Thank you for your time.

Meeting with the CPC Chair

Not long after I sent my email to the dean, Dr. Green officially recommended against promoting me. I tried to schedule a meeting with Dean Welsh to discuss my concerns further, but he declined. I also asked that the college promotion committee (CPC) members receive a copy of the letter I sent, and the dean initially agreed to do so. The CPC was the next faculty group to review my promotion application and issued its own recommendation to the dean. I thought it was important that every member of the promotion committee be informed of my allegations going forward. While I continued my efforts to meet with the dean, I met with the CPC chair to describe what I had discovered at that point.

Years before, the CPC chair had been a key figure who helped establish the Bush School at Texas A&M. He and I also served together as administrators under the previous dean, Ryan Crocker. I thought this personal connection would count for something. In fact, over the years, I discussed some difficulties I had with Dr. Ramsdel. So, he knew those issues very well. The CPC chair shared his own personal challenges in seeking full professorship, as well as his decision to withdraw when he realized he lacked his department's backing. This was a clever story. I was being subtly advised, once again, to withdraw my application. This was the second time that I had received this advice (with the first coming from Dr. Green, the department head), and it would not be the last. I was repeatedly asked, directly or indirectly, by multiple administrators to withdraw from consideration. That advice was based on an unwritten academic expectation that one should voluntarily exit the process at the hint of opposition from their colleagues. This was a classic academic tactic, framing retreat as an act of '*collegiality*' to avoid conflict, which in reality silences dissent. Interestingly, research suggests that such rules do not seem to apply to everyone. There is some evidence that some white professors are not held to such obligations and are often promoted even after being discouraged from applying.[11]

I also believed that I was being asked to withdraw to allow Texas A&M to wipe the record clean. Texas A&M would have ensured that the issues that were present in my promotion process would have never seen the light of day. This would have given the university plausible deniability to refute my claim that I experienced any problems in the process because it was never completed. I informed the CPC chair that I had no intention of withdrawing and that I was going to take my application and concerns all the way to the end.

EEOC Charge of Discrimination

Texas A&M's lack of plans to address my concerns about my treatment was becoming apparent to me. After failing to convince the university to address my concerns, I filed an EEOC charge. This prompted an external investigation of my full professor promotion process against the Bush School and Texas A&M. I no longer had confidence that my concerns were being taken seriously. I believed the university did not treat me the same as two recently promoted faculty members. So, I sought more information about the situation. Below was the EEOC charge I submitted.

Submitted EEOC Charge

> *I applied for promotion to full professor in my department. When my promotion was recommended to be denied, I inquired as to why and I was told by my department head, Dr. Green, it was for low performance. I filed a written formal complaint with Dean Welsh. Since the University opened, there has never been an African American full professor in the Bush School of Government and Public Affairs. I am also aware of other associate professors, outside my race, who had similar or lower performance, and they were promoted to full professor.*
>
> *I believe I was not promoted based on my race, Black, and I believe the reason given to me to be a pretext for discrimination.*

Difficulties Meeting the Dean

To keep them informed, I copied the Dean of Faculties (DOF) office on all email communications I had with Dean Mark Welsh. The DOF office oversaw the tenure and promotion process at Texas A&M and was among the first to be called in when problems arose. The DOF contacted me to arrange a meeting about my concerns after I had exchanged several emails with Welsh. Surprisingly, as soon as the DOF scheduled the meeting, they abruptly canceled it with little explanation. This cancellation followed an email exchange between Dean Welsh and me about his belief that there was still time to request a new set of external reviewer letters. Getting new letters would not solve the problem, as I understood it. The only real solution involved a new set of reviewer letters, the dismissal of Dr. Ramsdel as DPC chair, and a full acknowledgment of the contamination that entered my process. I was not interested in anything less or superficial, but I quickly learned that this was not something that the dean was willing to do. This exchange began when Dean Welsh forwarded the following email to me.

Emails between Dr. Bright, Dean Welsh, and DOF about Promotion Process Concerns

Leonard,

I met with the CPC chair yesterday to ensure he was familiar with your concerns about the process to date. He said you were able to express them to him yourself when you met with him over the holiday break. After speaking with him, I am confident he understands the complaints you registered with me over the last couple of weeks. I am also now reviewing the process by which the departmental committee collected the reviewer letters. If I determine it was done improperly or in a way intended to unduly influence the outcome of the review, DOF has assured me we will have time to solicit new letters. For now, the CPC chair is very comfortable with the process to date and the letters that his committee has available to review. They will meet as planned to consider your application.

After spending a great deal of time thinking through this, I am reversing course on my agreement to honor your request to give each member of the CPC a copy of the initial letter you sent to me outlining your complaints. I am not going to do that. I think it

Chapter 1: Situation

> *creates an impractical precedent, and I don't think it would be in the best interest of your deserved due process. I discussed this at some length with the DOF yesterday afternoon, and they agree. I know you meet with them this afternoon. I would encourage you to discuss this with them if you disagree.*

The following was my response.

> *Dean Welsh,*
>
> *Thank you for considering my request. I acknowledge your decision against submitting my rebuttals to the CPC and your confidence in the CPC chair's comfort with the process. I want to be clear that my complaint regarding Dr. Ramsdel concerns 1) the Bush School's process of allowing him to be the sole selector of the external letters and 2) including a person who has demonstrated hostility and animosity towards me. So far, I see no attempt at remediation of point 2. However, both issues (process and person) have placed my application at a disadvantage. Nonetheless, gathering additional letters is not agreeable to me. This will only expose me to additional review through no fault of my own. This is a problem that the Bush School allowed to happen. The damage has already been done, and additional letters will not rectify the damage. I will now await the CPC's recommendation and/or your decision before I decide my next steps on this one issue.*

15 minutes later, I received the following email from the DOF.

> *Based on your most recent email conversation with Dean Welsh, I do not see a clear indication at this time for meeting me tomorrow. I recommend we cancel the meeting.*

Welsh's refusal to inform the entire CPC of my complaints because it would present an unfair situation for me was interesting. This was an example of their attempt to maintain plausible deniability. This allowed the CPC to claim ignorance of my concerns, a defense against charges of wrongdoing. How can you charge the university with wrongdoing if you cannot show that those involved in the decisions were aware of complaints or of any potential wrongdoing that occurred? In fact, even at that point, the record already contained what occurred during my promotion process. They should have been aware of the efforts that Dr. Ramsdel, serving as the DPC chair, had made to contaminate the process. It was troubling to accept that anyone would express being *"very comfortable"* with what happened, unless they were a part of the scheme.

Meeting with Dean Welsh

One week after I met with the CPC chair, the committee voted unanimously against my application. This committee was composed of four faculty members appointed from the two departments at our college. The very next day after receiving this information, I requested that Dean Welsh make himself available to meet with me to discuss my concerns. Later that day, Dean Welsh and the Senior Executive Dean sat down for a face-to-face meeting with me and my wife. I was unaware that Christina had recorded it on her cell phone.[12]

From the very start, I asked why the Bush School had allowed someone with a documented history of problems with me to lead my promotion process. I also shared evidence that showed how Dr. Ramsdel may have sought to manipulate the external reviewer selection process as the DPC chair. Then, Christina described her experience working with Dr. Ramsdel. When he was interim department head, Dr. Ramsdel hired her as an adjunct. Two years later, he removed her from the position. This happened after a dispute with me, as the assistant dean. He then gave her class to another faculty member's wife.

Despite everything that Christina and I were describing, Dean Welsh was intent on communicating to me that I did not have his support. He claimed no one knew of the issues Christina and I had experienced with Dr. Ramsdel. He then tried to dismiss my complaints because I supposedly had not let them know sooner. When I stated I informed the department head of my concerns, in a turnaround, he then accused me of 'complaining too soon' and *"not allowing the process to play itself out."*

In the conversation, his senior executive dean, who is Black, acknowledged his own difficulty with achieving promotion to full professor at Texas A&M. Years earlier, he had applied but withdrew after learning that his department was in opposition. He attributed (at least partially) his failure to achieve full professorship to a *"racist"* faculty member and a sense of powerlessness to do anything about it. After this comment, Dean Welsh asked me, *"So, you are saying that Dr. Ramsdel is a racist, right?"* I replied, *"Who said that? I didn't say that."* In fact, I never used the terms racist or racism to describe any aspect of my experience at Texas A&M. Claims of racial discrimination do not automatically mean racism. In my opinion, using these terms distracts attention from provable, evidence-based disparities, and onto attitudes that are impossible to prove. Even more, I gave my complaints to Dean Welsh in writing, which centered on my belief that I had experienced racial discrimination, retaliation, and possibly even jealousy.

After more intense questioning from me, Dean Welsh contradicted his prior statement that no one knew of the hostilities that Dr. Ramsdel expressed towards me. He revealed that Dr. Ramsdel informed him and the DOF of multiple *"run-ins"* he had with me prior to acquiring approval to chair the DPC. After this revelation, I ended the meeting and forwarded the following email to Dean Welsh, copying the DOF and the provost, later that day.

Email from Dr. Bright to Dean Welsh about Face-to-Face Meeting

Dean Welsh,

After reflecting on our meeting today, I realize that you have been completely disingenuous. It was stunning that you knew that Dr. Ramsdel had acknowledged/discussed his potential conflicts of interest with the DOF at the beginning of my promotion process. You did not inform me of this despite my repeated written concerns and instead attempted to question the legitimacy of my concerns. Apparently, the DOF cleared him to participate as the chair of my department promotion committee purely on his side of the story. At the very least, I should have been informed about this from the beginning. Instead, I was kept in the dark. Had I been informed, I would have argued that he should have been recused because of our history. It is now clear that the DOF and the Bush School are working against me to protect this tainted and racially discriminatory promotion process. I filed a preliminary charge with the EEOC last week and will update my file with the information I learned today when they reopen for business.

Dean Welsh responded the next morning with the following email.

Leonard

To be clear, as part of my effort to address all of your allegations/concerns, I met with Dr. Ramsdel yesterday, one hour before I met with you and your wife. He has been out of the country. As I told you, he informed me that he had spoken with a member of the DOF staff to get advice on his involvement in reaching out to potential reviewers since the two of you had experienced run-ins in the past. The term "conflict of interest" is not something he said to me, nor did I use that phrase in our meeting yesterday. That is your characterization. I don't know exactly what words were used on that phone call. I wasn't a participant, nor was I aware of it earlier in your promotion process. As far as the rest of your note is concerned: (1) you have every right to pursue an EEOC and (2) I completely disagree with the conclusions you reached after our meeting. The executive associate dean and I are both prepared to

Chapter 1: Situation

share our thoughts on the meeting with the necessary parties if/when appropriate. Since you now allege that both DOF and the Bush School are working against you, I will speak with the DOF to determine who should communicate with you from this point forward.

Thanks again for your time yesterday.

Below was my email to the provost, quoting Dean Welsh's own words I transcribed from my wife's audio recording.

Email from Dr. Bright to Provost about Dean Welsh's Meeting

Provost,

The dean has parsed his words and escalated this situation. During our meeting, he stated:

"I talked with the DOF at great length about conflicts of interest, and they have differing views on what they are saying. The question is, if Dr. Ramsdel consulted with the DOF on the front end, which he did, and told them that he had some run-ins with you in the past, is it okay for me to be involved?"

Even more, he did not state that he had learned this from Dr. Ramsdel one hour before our meeting. Instead of solving this issue by acknowledging that Dr. Ramsdel should have recused himself (which even Dr. Ramsdel questioned), the dean has taken an adversarial position against me, investigated my credibility, and misrepresented the discussions of our meeting. I ask that the external reviewer letters obtained by Dr. Ramsdel be struck from my file because of a conflict of interest. I have evidence that supports the fact that Dr. Ramsdel sought to manipulate the selection of the external letters against me. I shared this information with the dean at my meeting yesterday.

According to written university policies, the dean, and the DOF had five days to report my complaints to the Office of Risk, Ethics, and Compliance (OREC). Neither the dean nor the DOF did this. The OREC investigated all internal allegations of discrimination, retaliation, and workplace harassment. It appeared to me that Welsh hoped to use my meeting with him to convince me to end my formal complaints. This was not going to happen. I had already filed my complaint with the EEOC before meeting with him and only announced that decision to them after the meeting as a courtesy. Upon learning of my EEOC complaint, the provost requested I contact the OREC office for an investigation into my discrimination allegations.

Texas A&M Discrimination Investigation

The DOF requested we meet to inform me that the provost had stopped my promotion process. After I asked about Dean Welsh's statement regarding Dr. Ramsdel's approval to chair the process, the DOF denied it. They pledged to follow up with me after their internal investigation. I received no follow-up. However, I got internal records where the DOF refuted Dr. Ramsdel's version of events. The DOF argued they did not approve of his participation. I also inquired whether the university was going to investigate my allegations of contamination in my promotion case, and they said that they had no plans to do so.

A few months later, the OREC investigators requested I meet with them to give a verbal statement about my racial discrimination, retaliation, and workplace harassment concerns. Before the process began, the OREC Director assured me they would approach the situation fairly and would inform me of their conclusions after they completed a thorough investigation. Based on his assurances, I reluctantly took part.

The Categorical Denial

The EEOC informed me that Texas A&M responded to my allegations of racial discrimination within days of receiving my complaint. Texas A&M denied, in no uncertain terms, that it discriminated or retaliated against me and requested the dismissal of my case, even before starting its investigation. In response, I sent the following email request to the OREC office and director:

Emails between Dr. Bright to OREC about Categorical Denial

Dear OREC Director,

I have been made aware by the EEOC that Texas A&M has categorically denied that it discriminated or retaliated against me. The allegation I made with the EEOC and with your office is one and the same. Please provide written clarification that Texas A&M rescinds its written position and will earnestly reserve its decision on my case until its internal investigation is complete.

The next day, I followed up with the following email:

Also, until I receive a satisfactory response to my request regarding Texas A&M's decision on my allegations, I will presume that its internal investigation has ended and will require no further comments from me.

The OREC office responded with the following email. Their response was a masterclass in bureaucratic deflection, confirming I could not trust them.

Dr. Bright,

You previously expressed concerns about Texas A&M's ability to conduct a fair and impartial internal investigation of the complaint you filed with my office since the Texas A&M System has already responded to the EEOC charge you filed. You stated that since the Texas A&M System had already denied your allegations to the EEOC, our internal investigation would not be fair. As you may or may not be aware, the EEOC demands a position statement from the defendant as soon as the charge is made. There are no delays allowed in conducting an investigation of the facts. Thus, the

> *Texas A&M System responded to your EEOC charge of discrimination based on a review of the evidence available at the time the response was made and concluded that the available evidence did not substantiate illegal race discrimination.*
>
> *The internal investigation conducted by the Office of Risk, Ethics, and Compliance (OREC) does not have to be conducted within the same strict timelines as the EEOC imposes. The internal investigators are currently attempting to obtain all the relevant facts and evidence. You have been given the opportunity to submit additional documents, facts, information, evidence, and relevant witnesses. We will provide the same opportunity to others involved. Once we have collected all the available information, we will look at the matter again and draw conclusions.*
>
> *We intend to proceed with our internal investigation.*

In no way did this response satisfy my concerns. The suggestion that the Texas A&M system was a separate entity from the OREC office from the standpoint of the EEOC was misleading. It was the responsibility of the Texas A&M system to respond on behalf of all departments and offices within the institution. The university was not prohibited from requesting more time, nor did it need to deny all allegations vehemently before completing a fair and thorough investigation. Their response to the EEOC confirmed I could not trust Texas A&M to be a neutral party. Their fervent argument was a public notice that the university intended to use its *"investigation"* to support its predetermined conclusion and desire to exonerate itself. So, I ended my participation.

The EEOC's Trove of Information

Besides providing me with Texas A&M's position statement, the EEOC also provided me with a treasure trove of documents about my promotion process. This included the committee deliberation memos produced by the department and college, the external reviewers' identities, and the letters they wrote. They also provided the transcripts of the OREC investigation interviews with each of the parties involved in my complaint. With this information in hand, I questioned whether my promotion process had been manipulated. It helped me sharpen my statement that Texas A&M failed to address effectively the problems that arose in my promotion process. I sent the provost an email to encourage her to start a proper investigation into my concerns.

Dr. Bright's Email to Provost about EEOC Information

Dear Provost,

The EEOC provided me with Texas A&M's position statement and all supporting documents to date. This new information has given me clear evidence that Texas A&M:

1. *Unethically relied on former employees of the Bush School as external reviewers who worked at the Bush School with professors Green, Ramsdel, and the CPC chair. Even more, this information was not disclosed in the department, department head, nor college committee deliberation letters in my file.*

2. *Produced discriminatory promotion reviews of my research that were inconsistent with statements made in previous annual reviews and a post-tenure review of my research performance. Texas A&M's prior annual and post-tenure reviews of my research took a very positive stance toward my journal quality, research impact, and publication numbers. At no point did Texas A&M ever conclude that my research performance did not meet departmental, college, or university expectations. The new conclusions that now label my research as "thin," "unimpactful," and "does not yet meet standards" are calculated codewords applied to me because of my race, and thus are a pretext to racial discrimination.*

3. *Did not obtain the required four reviewers from the Bush School's peer programs/universities. Texas A&M used two reviewers from the University of Georgia and two reviewers from American University, which subsequently intentionally quadrupled the number of negative reviewers. Also, most of the reviewers I submitted were dismissed with little to no explanation.*

As a Bush School faculty member, I find this new information embarrassing, and beneath the honor and integrity that President George H.W. Bush represented. The cumulative total of these discriminatory and unethical actions demonstrates I was not granted a fair, unbiased, and impartial full professor review. I alerted you that my promotion process was discriminatory and tainted, as well as my concerns about Dr. Ramsdel's involvement. You referred me to OREC to address my discrimination allegations. However, your internal investigation is now moot given that Texas A&M has formally denied my allegations to the EEOC and requested dismissal. As a result, I formally request that Texas A&M distance itself from those deplorable practices and take the following actions to resolve my case.

- *Reprimand and demote Dr. Green as department head.*
- *Reprimand Dr. Ramsdel.*
- *Provide a written apology to me.*
- *Grant my full professor promotion, which I have earned.*

Predictably, the provost went silent.

Surprise! No Discrimination Found.

Given the university's fervent categorical denial that it discriminated or retaliated against me, it was no surprise that its OREC office concluded that their "investigation" found no evidence of discrimination. Below, I summarize their statement.

Chapter 1: Situation

OREC Statement about Dr. Bright's Discrimination Allegations

> *There is no evidence to support Bright's allegation, and because Dr. Green and the Bush School provided legitimate, non-discriminatory reasons for recommending the denial of Bright's application for full professor, Investigators cannot conclude that Dr. Green and/or the Bush School discriminated against Bright based on race by using performance standards when recommending the denial of Bright's application for promotion that were not applied to other similarly situated faculty during their full promotion processes.*
>
> *Based on the totality of the circumstances, along with a thorough review of the evidence, investigators conclude that a preponderance of the evidence does not support that Dr. Green and/or the Bush School committed one or more acts of discrimination based on race against Dr. Leonard Bright, in violation of system policy. As a result, the allegation of discrimination based on race is unsubstantiated.*

One can question whether the university conducted anything close to a thorough investigation. In the documents that I obtained, the university's investigation did not consider the differences in the promotion process applied to me compared to two other promoted faculty members in my department. Their investigation was tantamount to asking Dean Welsh, and the faculty involved in my case to incriminate themselves, all while reminding them that admitting any wrongdoing came at significant risk to their continued employment at the university. It was unlikely that any rational individual would admit anything under those circumstances. Unsurprisingly, the investigators could find no one who would admit to engaging in discrimination and retaliation in my promotion case. That was certainly an open and shut investigation!

The Final Decision

Nine months beyond the normal promotion process, Dr. Michael Young (university president) notified me that he denied my promotion application. Then, a few months later, for reasons not fully explained, both the president and the provost left their positions. The university appointed Dr. Katherine Banks (as the new president) and a new provost.

Every committee member in the department and college voted against my application. I was expected to believe they had based their decisions on a thorough review of my achievement record. Academic culture argues that the judgement of these faculty members should not be questioned unless I had *"compelling reasons"* to reject them. There were obvious signs that something had gone very wrong. I discussed my concerns with a few faculty members and senior administrators to gain a better understanding of the situation. I would learn later that the university had evidence that confirmed my suspicions, but that they had willfully withheld it. Those I spoke with made concerted efforts to inform me that I had no support from them. They hoped that this messaging would lower my confidence, increase feelings of powerlessness, and increase fear of angering those who had the power to affect my future promotion chances. I resoundingly rejected these messages.

I always knew that achieving promotion to full professor would not be easy, and I was always open to advice about my path forward in achieving that goal. Also, I expected difficulty, considering few full professors nationally were Black. Even so, I expected similar treatment to how other promoted faculty members had been handled. The initial evidence I gathered suggested they treated me differently. There was much more that I would discover.

CHAPTER 2:
The Beginning

My first tenure-track position was at the University of South Alabama. I taught there for two years, and then for six years at the University of Louisville (UofL). While I was being considered for tenure and promotion at UofL, I applied for two tenured associate professor job openings at other universities. I entered the job market because of the discrimination and hostility I experienced at UofL, which prompted me to file an EEOC complaint. Even though UofL ultimately granted me tenure and promotion to associate professor, I went on the job market to explore other opportunities.

The Institution

I applied to Texas A&M University's Bush School of Government and Public Service. Texas A&M University is a public, land-grant, research university in College Station, Texas. The university began in 1876, and in 1948, it became the flagship institution of the Texas A&M University System. The institution has maintained close ties to the military, being one of six United States senior military colleges in the nation. Anyone who spends any length of time on its campus will recognize that Texas A&M is an institution steeped

Chapter 2: The Beginning

in tradition. Among the myriad symbols and expressions that define the Aggie culture, one stands out: "Gig 'em".[13]

A major addition to Texas A&M, the Bush School was founded in 1997 and named after the 41st President of the United States, George H. W. Bush. At the time of my application, the school only offered two master's degree programs. The school originated from the master's of public administration degree program housed in the political science department. When the school was founded, several members of the political science and economics departments were among the first faculty members to join its ranks.

The Bush School had established itself as a leading institution for training future leaders in public service and advancing knowledge and understanding of governance and policy issues. Their stated commitment to training public service professionals, and their motto that *"public service is a noble calling"* were important goals. However, on at least two occasions, I nearly withdrew my application. I wondered if a master's-only degree program was the best fit for me, especially since I was accustomed to teaching Ph.D. students at UofL. Also, I did not fancy living in Texas, especially given its political leanings and extremely hot weather. While on a job visit with another university, I received a message from the Bush School's program inviting me to an interview. So, I made my final decision regarding my future after I had the chance to meet with the faculty, students, and administrators at Texas A&M.

The Request and Offer

Given my performance record, I believed in my chances of leaving UofL, but I was not overly optimistic. I had some concerns about whether my decision to file an EEOC complaint against UofL would limit my ability to leave and gain another great academic position. These concerns were buried as I focused on my interview at the Bush School, which appeared to go well. After the interview, I received an email from a member of the department search committee informing me they needed my permission to speak formally with my department chair at UofL. This request quickly brought my concerns about my decision to file an EEOC complaint and my negative experiences with my department at UofL to the foreground of my mind. I considered how I should navigate this request. Even though I had serious issues with my department colleagues, my promotion application had the support of my dean, and I believed that the provost and university president would follow suit. So, I delicately asked if she could contact the dean of the college instead of the department chair. She stated she would not contact the department chair, but quickly warned that in her experience, the word often gets out, eventually. She stated that *"Faculty talk to other faculty."*

On New Year's Day, I received an email from the Bush School's program department head, Dr. Hopkins, wishing me a Happy New Year. He offered me the position at Texas A&M and informed me that the department had voted overwhelmingly to extend me a job offer, though they had not yet voted on the question of tenure.

Faculty Talked

Happily, I tentatively accepted Texas A&M's job offer pending that the final offer included tenure, the rank of associate professor, and an agreeable salary. I was told that since the tenure process was not completed at UofL, Texas A&M required that I also undergo a concurrent tenure review with them. So, I submitted my promotion dossier and awaited the decision from Texas A&M's Board of Regents before even considering submitting a notice of resignation to UofL.

Several weeks later, Dr. Hopkins informed me that there was now some resistance among the Bush School senior faculty members regarding granting me tenure, even though they had voted overwhelmingly in favor of extending me the employment offer. He did not go into detail about their decision. Years later,

Chapter 2: The Beginning

I learned that the concern among the faculty was more serious than I had known. The Department Promotion Committee (DPC) chair sent the following email to the dean describing its recommendation regarding my case.

Email from DPC Chair to Dean Crocker about Dr. Bright's Tenure Vote Results

> *This afternoon, the department promotion committee (DPC) met to discuss the case of Leonard Bright. Eleven of the twelve tenured faculty members were present.*
>
> *By a vote of 8 to 3, the committee voted against the conferral of tenure for Bright. There was a general feeling that the existing research record at this point in time does not warrant tenure for a school with our aspirations.*
>
> *The committee held a second vote as to whether he should be offered an untenured associate professor position, and the vote was 10 yes, 1 no. The consensus was that he had the potential to publish in the two leading journals in the field (Public Administration Review and the Journal of Public Administration Research and Theory) and that after he had demonstrated this competency, we would be comfortable moving his rank to associate professor with tenure.*

This was astounding. To be clear, I had already achieved a national reputation for my research on public service motivation. There was no disputing the fact that my research appeared in highly ranked journals, and that the citations of my research were well above average. However, the department faculty held the belief that tenure and promotion in my case should hinge on two specific general-field journals.

Interestingly, around this same time, my department head at UofL began emailing me that he was aware of my application to Texas A&M and demanded that I formally confirm my intentions to leave. Certainly, he did not learn about my application from me. Nonetheless, the news about my application was out. It confirmed that someone at Texas A&M did indeed talk to someone at UofL. Given this situation, I concluded that if I had to rely on the recommendations of people who I considered to be my enemies, I would remain at UofL for the indefinite future.

The Defense of the Record

The Bush School faculty's unusual recommendation to withhold tenure or promotion to associate professor to two of the dozens of journals in my field was not the final decision in my case. First off, equating research competency with particular journals instead of the content of the research is problematic, given the outsized role that professional networks and luck play in such outcomes[14]. Most of the faculty involved in that decision had never published in these general-field journals themselves, much less faced a requirement to do so during their tenure processes. In fact, in all my years as a faculty member at Texas A&M, this requirement has never been applied to any promotion or tenure case I was a part of. Of the very few professors who had published in those journals, most did so years after they were promoted to full professor. Thankfully, Dr. Hopkins directly and forcefully addressed this inconsistency in an extensive memo to Dean Crocker. Dr. Hopkins' memo masterfully countered the committee's recommendations (see Appendix B for Dr. Hopkin's full memo).

Dr. Hopkins' memo explained that I emerged as a strong candidate during the Bush School's national search for a faculty position in public administration/public management, which drew 52 applicants. Although I was initially ranked second by the search committee, I was offered the position after their first-choice candidate declined. Dr. Hopkins believed that my request to be tenured and promoted to associate professor was strongly supported by my qualifications and extensive documentation, including my tenure packet and 17 very positive external recommendation letters. While the DPC voted in favor of promotion without tenure, this was a rare and discouraged practice at Texas A&M. The memo noted that the DPC's rationale was focused narrowly on the placement of my publications, overlooking the Bush School's broader standards of excellence in teaching, research, and service. He argued that my record reflected consistent strength across all three areas. Dean Crocker concurred with Dr. Hopkins' assessment and capped his support with the following memo.

Dean Crocker's Memo to the Provost Supporting Dr. Bright's Tenure and Promotion to Associate Professor

Dear Provost,

Dr. Bright's candidacy is the product of an extensive national search yielding a highly qualified and diverse pool of applicants. His appointment to the faculty has been strongly recommended by the Search Committee, the department head and the general faculty of the Bush School, and his appointment with tenure on arrival has been strongly recommended by the department head, an action with which I concur. Although strongly supportive of his appointment to the faculty as associate professor (10 yes: 1 no), promotion committee was instructed improperly to also consider the possibility of an appointment as associate professor without tenure (3 yes: 8 no). This option has not been practiced in the School, it would not be congruent with the strong preference to link the rank of associate professor with tenure at Texas A&M, and it does not fit with those few cases where exceptions might be granted due to the absence of documented prior performance and experience in one or more of the areas relevant to tenure (teaching, research, service).

I am sure that Dean Crocker's decision was not taken kindly by some of the faculty in the department. Still, the entire situation suggested to me that the faculty members at Texas A&M did indeed talk to the faculty members at UofL. Perhaps after learning of my experiences at UofL, some members of the Bush School faculty attempted to create a less-than-ideal job offer to kill the deal, hoping I would decline it. The strategy they used to make that happen is the *chase-your-tail journal game*. This is a tried-and-true academia-wide ploy used against non-supported faculty in the tenure and promotion process. It involved a search for journals that the promotion and/or tenure candidate had not published in and then advanced a claim that publications in those specific journals are requirements for tenure and promotion. The faculty used the fact that I had no publications in two of the dozens of ranked journals in my field, which contradicted the fact that no such standard existed in the Bush School and differed noticeably from how they treated other promoted faculty in their department.

Years later, I learned that the candidate the department prioritized as their first choice for the position was a doctoral student who was nearing the completion of her degree program. She had no prior experience as a tenured track professor, had little to no published research, and ultimately had no proven record of academic achievement. Some may suggest that it is not unusual for some departments to prioritize candidates with little to no experience over those who are more experienced. Less experienced professors are more malleable than experienced ones, who have an established trajectory. Their problem arose when their first choice declined their offer, and then the department reasoned that I should be offered employment terms that were more consistent with the accomplishments of a newly minted junior faculty. I had eight years of experience in tenure-track academic positions, multiple publications in highly ranked journals in my field, and years of experience in senior academic leadership positions.

The inconsistencies between the DPC's reasoning, the written promotion standards, and past practices may have been the primary reasons they lost their attempt to deny me tenure. I accepted their job offer and hoped that any concerns that the faculty members had would recede. Unfortunately, this was not the case. Some members of the faculty would resurrect this same specific strategy years later under new department and Bush School leadership when I sought promotion to the full professor rank.

My First Seven Years and Leadership Opportunities

During my first seven years, I kept myself busy at work and at home. My wife and I bought undeveloped land, cleared it, and built our home with our own hands. Besides my home life, I worked diligently and selflessly in my department. I was committed to advancing my research in public management, attending academic conferences in my field, and extending my survey research of local and state government employees. My success at the Bush School led to opportunities to engage in senior-level leadership positions at the college and university levels. The first opportunity came at the beginning of my third year when Ambassador Ryan Crocker returned to his position as the dean from his service in President Barack Obama's Administration. He appointed me to serve as his assistant dean of graduate education at the Bush School.

Certainly, a few of my colleagues were not happy with my appointment as assistant dean, even though I served as an assistant director at South Alabama, a president of a regional professional association at UofL, and a president of a state-level professional association in my field. Despite my experience and qualifications, some faculty members openly questioned whether I was selected purely because of my race and argued that other, more senior faculty members in the department were overlooked. One faculty member even expressed to my wife, who was an adjunct professor in my department, that, *'if the dean wanted a Black administrator, he should have promoted a Black faculty in the department that they knew better.'* I brushed this off as simple jealousy, but the underlying hostility that was always there emerged.

Conflicts with an Interim Department Head

My appointment as assistant dean was announced to the department. Dr. Hopkins, the department head, was away on leave. Dr. Ramsdel, a long-serving faculty member, was appointed as the interim department head during his absence. He expressed disappointment with my administrative appointment, became a major source of conflict in my role as assistant dean, and challenged my role openly and repeatedly. He readily commented that I was *"only brought here to be a faculty."* After one dispute, he visited my office to inform me he was reassigning my wife's class to the wife of another faculty member. Ironically, one year earlier, it was he who had asked my wife to develop that very class. My wife and I strongly believed that his sudden decision to dismiss her was motivated by anger over his disagreement with my role as assistant dean, given that she had had no negative interactions with him.

Eventually, my wife emailed Dean Crocker describing the treatment she experienced from Dr. Ramsdel. The dean investigated the issue, confirmed her account of the situation, apologized to her for what she had experienced, and offered her the opportunity to return, which she declined. While the dean had the power to force Dr. Ramsdel to rehire her, we did not believe this was a productive course of action, given the level of hostility Dr. Ramsdel had displayed toward us. I felt that her return would have exposed her to more mistreatment. Unexpectedly, three months later, it was announced that Dr. Ramsdel was out as the interim department head and that Dr. Hopkins was returning to his position.

Chapter 2: The Beginning

New Leadership Emerged

After the retirement of Dean Crocker, Mark Welsh was hired as the dean of the Bush School. The Bush School's deans differed from the typical deans of major schools of public affairs. Most were internationally known, did not have prior experience as a tenured faculty member, had little to no experience in senior academic leadership positions, and did not possess a doctorate degree. The appointment of Mark Welsh followed that tradition. He was a retired United States Air Force four-star general. Prior to his appointment, he served as Chief of Staff of the United States Air Force and a member of the Joint Chiefs of Staff in President Obama's Administration.

Similarly, department leadership also underwent transitions. One year after returning to his position as department head, Dr. Hopkins retired from the university. Dr. Johnson was appointed the interim department head until Dr. Green, an internal candidate, was hired as the permanent department head. Now that Crocker had retired, the appointments of Mark Welsh as the dean and Dr. Green as the department head gave the faculty new opportunities to settle old scores. These leadership changes were followed by a new era of workplace hostility marked by multiple formal grievances, EEOC investigations, and a lawsuit brought by me.

Unfortunately, the support I received in the past did not go over well with a few of the senior department faculty members who were awaiting their opportunities to strike back. Those opportunities finally came years later under a new dean and department head. In fact, one of the most disruptive characteristics of the Bush School's work environment was the high level of turnover among the senior leaders of my department and college. Over my first seven years as a faculty member at the Bush School, I served under three deans and four department heads. This level of turnover was disruptive and became a pathway that was used to undo what previous decision makers had done.

CHAPTER 3:

The Contamination

After serving as an associate professor and assistant dean for a few years, I was offered a position as an assistant provost in the graduate school. I served in that role for a couple of years before I stepped down and returned to my full-time faculty position. It was time for a change. I also wanted to prepare for the next stage of my career.

Over the past year, my department promoted two professors to the rank of full professor. Based on their vitas and my understanding of their accomplishments, my performance was similar. Interestingly, all three of us had served in one administrative role or another, with the only difference being that their administrative roles were limited to the department level, while mine were at the college and university levels. Even more, my annual and post-tenure reviews consistently communicated that my accomplishments always met or exceeded the department's expectations. At no point were any deficiencies highlighted regarding my performance at any level. Still, I understood that achieving the full professor rank would not come easy, and the hostility and jealousy that were present among some of the faculty would not make it easier.

While I hoped that most of the faculty would conduct a fair review, I had to face the realization that some faculty members might work to thwart my application for promotion. I discussed my plans with Dr. Hopkins over lunch before he retired. He encouraged me to proceed, but only after I discussed my plans with the full professors in the department.

Discussion with Senior Faculty

The following year, after Dr. Hopkins retired, Dr. Johnson was appointed acting department head, as a national search was underway. I followed Dr. Hopkins' advice and discussed my plans with every full professor in the department before I applied for promotion. I wanted to make sure that I gave them the opportunity to inform me of any weaknesses in my record regarding the written department promotion standards. The feedback I received was positive. In hindsight, I came to realize that the faculty were not forthcoming in their plans. The only faculty member who communicated opposition was Dr. Ramsdel, the former interim department head, who had dismissed my wife from her adjunct position in what I believed was an act of hostility.

Interestingly, in response to my initial email requesting a meeting to discuss my plans to seek full professor, Dr. Ramsdel replied that he *"knew"* that I was considering applying for promotion. He revealed he had already begun soliciting external reviewers for my case, months earlier, before I had even decided for myself or discussed the possibility with the department. It was also very clear from our conversation that he disagreed with my plans. Other faculty members, he commented, would also express similar sentiments. When I told him he was the only faculty member to express his negative viewpoint, he retorted that *he would recuse himself* from the process. However, after I announced my final decision to seek promotion to the department, I was stunned to learn that he had been appointed to serve as the chair of my promotion process, instead of recusing himself. I learned later that he lobbied the department, college, and university officials for the position. When I learned of Dr. Ramsdel's appointment, I immediately voiced my concerns to Dr. Johnson, the acting department head. Dr. Johnson assured me he would discuss the matter with the dean's office. However, to ensure that my promotion case continued to move forward, I tried to work with Dr. Ramsdel. Unsurprisingly, it did not go well.

Promotion Process and Rules

The promotion process at Texas A&M was multi-staged. It began with the development of my dossier, which included my cover letter, supporting documents, proposed lists of external reviewers, and a list of reviewers that should not be contacted. After my dossier was submitted, Texas A&M was one of the few universities that did not allow candidates to review or rebut any of the external letters obtained, nor the deliberation memos produced by the department, college, and other decision makers. The only right that the candidates had was that they *"should be advised, by the department head, of the recommendation for or against promotion and/or tenure at each level of review."* Nonetheless, the use of *"should"* suggested that even this right was not assured. As I will show later, I was not informed of the status of my case at each level of the review process, after I complained about the process and my treatment. I submitted my full promotion cover letter (see Appendix C for my full cover letter) and my proposed external reviewers to Dr. Ramsdel and then I awaited the mandatory updates and the final decision on my case from the university.

The Peer Reviewer Process

A bedrock norm of the academic promotion process is the use of evaluators who are experts in the specialty field of the professor under evaluation. This is a quality control measure that ensures that evaluation feedback comes from individuals qualified to provide that information. The strength and legitimacy of the peer review process are based on its perceived use of experts who exercise fairness and impartiality. Violations of these expectations will corrupt the entire promotion process.

To boost fairness and credibility, peer reviewers are internal and external. Internal peer reviewers typically involve qualified individuals employed within the candidate's home department or university, whereas external peer reviewers are solicited from outside the university. While internal peer reviewer feedback is an important aspect of the promotion process, external reviewer feedback is heavily relied upon by faculty and university decision makers.

Texas A&M Promotion Rules

Texas A&M required a minimum of five external reviewers to be involved in the promotion process. In my case, six external full professors[15] were selected to serve as external reviewers (see Appendix D for the external reviewer letters collected). The solicitation for these reviewers started with the gathering of a list of 10 from me given to the department promotion committee (DPC) chair, who also created his own list of 10 on the department's behalf. Typically, once the reviewers agree to serve, the promotion dossier is forwarded to them with a request for them to return their evaluation within a certain period. However, some researchers have found that most universities offered few instructions,[16] whereas others found these instructions varied broadly from university to university.[17] Most times, the reviewers are asked to comment on the contribution/importance of the candidate's research, the quality of the candidate's publications, and their future trajectory.

Most promotion process rules ensure that the external reviewers selected are independent from the candidates being reviewed and thus prohibit the use of reviewers closely affiliated with the candidate. Unfortunately, much less attention has been given to the undue influence that department faculty can have on who is selected to provide reviews. Some universities have policies in place that attempt to address this situation. For instance, there are universities that require external reviewer solicitations to be conducted by college representatives rather than by the department faculty. For example, the University of Georgia's promotion policies prohibit the *"head of the promotion/tenure unit and other eligible voting faculty in the unit"* from contacting external reviewers about their promotion candidates. Similarly, other universities give the candidates the right to review their department's proposed external reviewer list to address proactively any concerns that candidates may have about the fit of the department's choices with their field of expertise. Unfortunately, neither of these practices was used at Texas A&M, which I believe contributed to the controversy that engulfed my promotion process.

The Solicitation Guidelines

Each year, Texas A&M published guidelines for promotion cases. These guidelines address expectations regarding the composition of the promotion dossier, the evaluation process, and the external reviewers' solicitation process. These guidelines were very explicit about the requirement that external reviewers were to be independent, *"arm's-length,"* and pose *"no conflict of interest"* regarding the candidate seeking promotion. However, the guidelines were silent on the extent to which reviewers should be an *"arm's length"* from the department to ensure independence, nor did they give the candidates any right to be informed of the department's choices. To further enforce the *"arm's length"* rule with respect to the candidate only, the guidelines stated that the ideal reviewer should not be,

- *within 5 to 10 years of last collaboration or co-authorship with the candidate.*
- *from the same institution where the candidate worked previously.*
- *from the same institution where the candidate obtained their terminal degree.*

- *from a previous advisor, mentor, or committee member of the candidate.*

While the guidelines were heavily focused on ensuring that the candidate was not advantaged, there were a few that addressed the expectations of the reviewers the department should select. For example, the guidelines stated that the department should *"take care"* to avoid using reviewers *"whose objectivity is open to challenge."* In addition, below are several other guidelines highlighted.

- *If possible, do not include more than one letter from the same institution.*
- *The file should still include at least four letters from individuals in peer programs/universities.*
- *It is recommended that an equal number of letters be solicited for all candidates.*
- *A lack of response from a reviewer who has been asked to send a letter should not be interpreted as a negative statement against the candidate.*

Texas A&M Solicitation Letter

The solicitation letter template used during my promotion process at Texas A&M for the Bush School of Government can be found in Appendix E. Although the template stated that promotion depend on teaching, research, and service, the reviewer questions focused only on my research productivity. While the university did not prohibit questions that elicited assessments of my teaching and service accomplishments, my department did not take advantage of that opportunity. This was important given that 70% of my workload at Texas A&M centered on teaching and service. Thus, while research was an important dimension for promotion, it only accounted for 30% of my work effort. So, to ask external reviewers to determine whether I should be recommended for promotion based only on 30% of my work effort was troubling.

DPC Chair Solicitation Activities

Again, Texas A&M's promotion guidelines provided candidates with little to no protection from undue department influence regarding the selection of external reviewers. My case showed the damage that this practice had on my promotion process. It was irresponsible for Texas A&M to let Dr. Ramsdel, who had a history of animosity towards me and my wife, lead the selection of my external reviewers. Problems immediately emerged regarding how Dr. Ramsdel interacted and communicated with potential external reviewers.

Let's be Strategic!

At the very beginning of my promotion process, I received an email from Dr. Ramsdel that essentially asked me to help him work around the promotion process rules. This request occurred after I emailed announcing my decision to apply for promotion. Below was the email exchange of that conversation.

Emails between Dr. Bright and Dr. Ramsdel about Promotion Application

Professor Bright	*I have notified you and the department of my intention to seek promotion to full professor this year. Can you tell me the department deadlines for my files?*
Dr. Ramsdel	*The deadline for submission of your materials is July 1, but I would like to start soliciting external reviewers around the first of June. Some invitations will come from a list that you provide, and the department head and I will come up with our own list in consultations with other professors as appropriate. You can also identify people that you don't want us*

Chapter 3: The Contamination

	to invite. We might talk about the best way for you to approach this strategically. Let me know if you have other questions.
Professor Bright	*I will work on my list and have it to you within 2 weeks. Will this work? Also, will you need my cover letter before the reviewers are solicited?*
Dr. Ramsdel	*That's fine, Leonard. As a strategic consideration, you might want to leave some people off your list who you think would provide favorable reviews. This goal is to get at least three people from each list to agree to write these letters. These can't be people that you have worked with or studied under, by the way.*

The discussion showed how securing outside reviewers could be manipulated, possibly benefitting or hindering those under review. Dr. Ramsdel's request that I *"leave some people off [my] list who [I] think would provide favorable reviews"* was an invitation to help him circumvent the process *supposedly* in my favor. I did not comply.

Difficulty Finding Reviewers

A few days after I forwarded my list of proposed external reviewers to Dr. Ramsdel and my refusal to coordinate the development of my list, he insisted he was having difficulty finding people to serve as external reviewers. Below is the email exchange I had with Dr. Ramsdel regarding this issue.

Email between Dr. Bright and Dr. Ramsdel about the External Reviewers Qualifications

Dr. Ramsdel	*I am having a hard time finding people on your list who are able to serve as external reviewers (that's why I wanted to start this process early). Can you provide a few more names? They should be prominent scholars who are full professors and preferably at*

> *research institutions that are comparable to Texas A&M or who are otherwise in top public administration departments with strong research orientations.*

Professor Bright *As requested, attached are three additional reviewers. Also, you indicated [during a phone call] that you had not contacted everyone on my list. I want to reiterate that according to the DOF, NASPAA[18] accreditation status can be used as one peer indicator, in combination with others. Certainly, not every NASPAA school would be considered our peers, especially from the standpoint of their research 1 status and rank. The attached revised list is based on NASPAA status, U.S. News rank, and research 1 status.*

The very next day that Dr. Ramsdel sent me an email lamenting having difficulties finding reviewers, I later learned that he had already secured most of his reviewers and had rejected most of mine. A few days later, after he had secured the participation of six external reviewers, none of them were taken from my second proposed list.

The Campaign

The discussion that follows provides a detailed account of the email campaign Dr. Ramsdel had with several potential reviewers, where he communicated his disagreement with my decision to seek promotion and made other damaging statements. I obtained this information from the EEOC and through discovery requests.

The email records between Dr. Ramsdel, and potential external reviewers were revealing. They raise questions as to whether Dr. Ramsdel's communication strategy with several external reviewers compromised their independence. Texas A&M's guidelines stated

Chapter 3: The Contamination

that, *"When requesting letters, please use email and clearly state in the subject of the message the request."* This policy practice ensured that a written record of all communications with reviewers was maintained to monitor any inappropriate communication. While the email record between Dr. Ramsdel and the potential external reviewers was far from complete, it showed that Dr. Ramsdel may not have followed this protocol. For example, when asked to provide a copy of all communications he had with the reviewers, here was his response.

Email between Dr. Ramsdel and Department Secretary about Communications with Reviewers

Dr. Ramsdel   *I will forward those email invitations and responses that I still have to you and Linda, as I find them. I do not have all the ones I sent, as I mentioned, and some of the responses came over the phone rather than via email. All the email invitations were nearly identical in their language, except that I might said something like "how's Jenny" or "what about those Red Sox" if it was someone I knew. Also mentioned, I originally approached Reviewer 2 at a conference when I was anticipating that Leonard would put himself up for promotion.*

This email alone showed that Texas A&M administrators were fully aware (at some point) of potential problems with Dr. Ramsdel's practices. Yet, the process proceeded full steam ahead. The lack of oversight was so egregious that Dr. Ramsdel had no concerns about revealing on the record that he had even *"approached* [tampered with] *Reviewer 2"* months before I initiated the promotion process.

Again, the importance that all communication with external reviewers be conducted in writing was not prioritized. I was not given any documentation of the initial request to three of the six reviewers used. The record also suggested that both the potential external reviewers and Dr. Ramsdel readily engaged in private conversations outside of the view of writing and the reach of accountability. Some of these private conversations resulted in declines or agreements to participate immediately afterwards. Below are a few examples.

Email between Dr. Ramsdel and a Potential External Reviewer

Dr. Ramsdel   *Dear [Potential Reviewer]*

The Bush School's department will be considering Leonard Bright for promotion to full professor this fall. Outside letters from prominent scholars play an important role in our deliberations, and we would be grateful in this regard if you could assess his research accomplishments. His c.v. is attached.

Thanks for considering this request.

Potential Reviewer   *Hi Dr. Ramsdel, can we talk about this?*

Dr. Ramsdel   *Sure. Give me a number and time to call or you can call me. I am in San Diego but am working most of the day.*

Record of telephone conversation not disclosed

Potential Reviewer   *Dr. Ramsdel, I'm sorry. I'm going to pass on this.*

Email between Dr. Ramsdel and a Reviewer 4

Reviewer 4   *Hi Dr. Ramsdel, I hope you are well. I just left a message for you on your phone. I will be glad to write a letter on Leonard Bright's record, but I wanted to speak with you briefly. I'll try to reach you again, or you can get me.*

Chapter 3: The Contamination

Record of telephone conversation not disclosed

Dr. Ramsdel   Email to Department Head

> *Talked to [Reviewer 4] a few minutes ago, and he agreed to write a review.*

While I could not get the record of the private conversation between Dr. Ramsdel and Reviewer 4, this reviewer wrote a negative assessment that I should not receive promotion.

The next exchange provided clues about the information that Dr. Ramsdel may have been sharing with potential reviewers during his private conversations. In the following exchange, Dr. Ramsdel told a potential reviewer not to consider my administrative workload in his assessments of my research accomplishments and apparently told him I was advised not to pursue promotion. These comments clearly impacted the potential reviewer's decision to refuse participation.

Email between Dr. Ramsdel and a Potential External Reviewer

Dr. Ramsdel   *I hope things are going well. We will be considering Leonard Bright for promotion to full professor this fall. Outside letters from prominent scholars play an important role in our deliberations, and we would be grateful in this regard if you could assess his research accomplishments. His c.v. is attached. Thanks for considering this request.*

Potential Reviewer   *Thank you for the message and the invitation to review Len's promotion materials. Can I have a day to think about this? I have committed to do 2 other reviews already, though the timelines for completion are somewhat staggered. Also, can you confirm that*

> Leonard's work there has largely been administrative (with his roles at Bush and now the Graduate School)? I think that context may be important to understanding/framing his research productivity there.

Dr. Ramsdel   *Thanks. Leonard's administrative responsibilities have been part time, and he has been compensated with reduced teaching loads and relief from departmental service. There is not an expectation that they be taken into account in evaluating his research record.*

Dr. Ramsdel   *I also should have mentioned that I would be happy to answer any questions over the phone if that is helpful.*

Record of telephone conversation not disclosed

Potential Reviewer   *I am sorry, but I am going to pass on this opportunity. As I noted, I have committed to do a couple of tenure reviews already but, given that I had familiarity with Leonard's record (which I reviewed at the point of his initial appointment at A&M), I wanted to help if I could.*

Off-the-record: my sense, uninformed as it is from your context and what he has been advised is that it may be a little early for him to be going up.

I hate to say no, but I hope you understand.

At least two of the reviewers (i.e., Reviewers 3 and 5) agreed to participate and were willing to modify their involvement and even their review letters to satisfy Dr. Ramsdel's wishes. For example, in the exchange below, Reviewer 3 suggested that he could recall the assessment he delivered and revise it to suit the needs of Dr. Ramsdel.

Chapter 3: The Contamination

Email between Dr. Ramsdel and External Reviewer 3

Reviewer 3 — *Dr. Ramsdel, attached is my letter about Professor Bright. I am going to wait to submit it in response to the staff person's letter, or wherever the guidelines direct me to submit it. If you need something different, please let me know. I hope all is going well for you.*

All best wishes

Dr. Ramsdel — *Thanks very much. I really appreciate your willingness to do this, and I don't think you need to do anything more. I will forward your letter to Cindy, and she will put it in the DPC file.*

I hope you are doing well. Things are fine with my family, and I am healthy and treated better than I deserve at work.

Reviewer 3 — *Thanks very much for your response, I appreciate it more than you might realize. I was hoping the letter is appropriate to your needs. I know that you do not intend to steer or influence the letters, but this is a sensitive letter to write, and I want to get it right as best I can. I have to call it like I see it, as I am sure you understand. I wondered if the last sentence of the letter is a bit much but given the gist of the letter I wanted to express the sincerity of my intent. Let me know if you would like me to soften that last sentence a bit...*

Dr. Ramsdel — *Your letter is perfectly appropriate. I would be happy to give you a call about that.*

Reviewer 3 was a well-known scholar in my field, whom I had included on my list of potential reviewers and who had frequently referenced my research. However, this interaction raises questions that centered on whether his close association with Dr.

Ramsdel impacted his objectivity. Prior to this exchange, I was unaware of the closeness between Reviewer 3 and Dr. Ramsdel. Nor was I informed that Reviewer 3 and another of his colleagues (Reviewer 4) from his same department were used in contradiction to university policies against "*double-stacking.*"

Next, in another exchange, Reviewer 5 suggested that he could withdraw his agreement to conduct the review if that would bolster Dr. Ramsdel's argument that no one wanted to serve as an external reviewer in my promotion process.

Email between Dr. Ramsdel and External Reviewer 5

Reviewer 5 *I don't know if you've checked, but I went to google scholar and the person we spoke about had about 1200 citations! Some of the big foots cited this person's research, so they might be other persons to contact. One article has 400 citations. Doesn't make a career or case, for sure, but I thought this might help.*

Dr. Ramsdel *I saw that too, and it's the best case that can be made. I have been reaching out to some of those people but no luck so far.*

Reviewer 5 *Ok, good, I assumed you had checked it out and might be contacting them. Maybe that is a way out of this, that no one is willing to review the case says something, right? I wouldn't be offended if you needed to pull me out to make it unanimous.*

Reviewer 5 ultimately participated in the process after this exchange. Apparently, Dr. Ramsdel also had a very close friendship with Reviewer 5. They co-authored at least two publications and were co-workers at the Bush School years earlier. It just so happened that Reviewer 5 worked at the same university and in the same department as Reviewer 6, in contradiction, once again, to university policies against *"double-stacking."*

Notably, Reviewer 5 was the former editor of one of the two general-field journals the department attempted to require of me during my hiring process. I interacted with him when he was the editor of that journal approximately ten years prior. He rejected a manuscript I had submitted, citing that the reviewers' recommendations (although all strongly supportive of publication) were not sufficiently compelling in his view. In the same year, Reviewer 5 published his own article (as editor) on a closely related topic with a similar title in that very journal.[19] Now, serving as a reviewer in my promotion process, Reviewer 5 questioned if I had *"deliberately targeted"* lower-ranked general field journals to increase my number of publications (and apparently my high citations), which he mentioned in his recommendation against my promotion.

The Smoking Gun

Was the strategy my department used to solicit the external reviewers tantamount to collusion? On the day he ended the solicitation process, Dr. Ramsdel expressed his confidence that the reviewers he knew and selected would not let him down. See the exchange below.

Email between Dr. Ramsdel and Dr. Green (Department Head)

Dr. Ramsdel   *Here is a second acceptance from Leonard's list, and it gives us a total of five. [Reviewer 5] is very well-regarded as a PA [Public Administration] scholar.*

Dr. Green   *Excellent! Do you see the need to seek out additional letters at this time?*

> Dr. Ramsdel *I would prefer to wait now that we have five, four of whom I know and won't let us down.*

The department's decision to end the solicitation process occurred one week after it started. Even more, they believed they had assurances that the reviewers would support their perspective. Surprisingly, the reviewers' assessments of my research were mixed for several reasons that will be addressed in the following discussion.

The Characteristics of the External Reviewers

Multiple Misaligned Reviewers

Table 1 shows that the external reviewers used in my promotion process were not all centered in my fields of public management, public service motivation, and/or higher education. This was problematic given Texas A&M's guidelines, which stated that *"outside reviewers' letters allow an opportunity for authorities in the candidate's field to evaluate the candidate's accomplishments and potential."* Using reviewers who were not scholars in my field violated these expectations.

On the one hand, Reviewers 1 and 2 illustrated the best understanding of my research accomplishments. These reviewers were active scholars in my field of public management, and I was familiar with their work as well.[20] Reviewers 4 and 5 were general-field public administration/political science scholars. These reviewers were closely aligned with Dr. Ramsdel's field of research, not mine. This solicitation strategy produced conflicting opinions about my research accomplishments, especially between the public management[21] and the public administration/political science reviewers. As a result, Reviewers 1 and 2 (public management scholars) argued that I should receive promotion, while Reviewers 4 and 5 (public administration/political science scholars) argued that I should not.

TABLE 1

External Reviewers by Rank, Research Field, and Place of Work

Reviewer	Rank	Research Field	Place of Work
1	Professor	Public Management	University of Miami
2	Professor	Public Management	Georgetown University
3	Professor	Public Administration, Political Science/Public Management	University of Georgia
4	Professor	Political Science	University of Georgia
5	Professor	Public Administration, Political Science	American University
6	Professor	Public Management	American University

In addition, the misalignments between the external reviewers and my promotion application can also be questioned from the extent to which the home universities, departments, and programs of the external reviewers were peers of Texas A&M, the Bush School, and my department. Texas A&M's tenure and promotion policies stated that among the minimum of five letters that can be used in the promotion process, *"at least four letters [should be] from individuals in peer programs/universities* [22]*."* This does not appear to have been followed.

My department of public service was ranked in the top 30-40 programs in public affairs, at best. Most of the reviewers chosen were employed in programs ranked among the top 10 programs in the nation. Given this misalignment, it was unclear whether the external reviewers were providing an assessment using the promotion standards promulgated at the Bush School, or the promotion criteria adopted by their own esteemed departments. At the time of my promotion application, the Bush School was a master's-only degree program that was home to only two degrees, in international affairs and public service. None of the Bush School's programs or departments taught undergraduates or doctoral students.

Hence, faculty in my department were expected to contribute the lion's share of their time to teaching, which accounted for 60% of our work effort. I seriously doubt that the external reviewers considered these facts as they were reviewing my promotion file. For example, Reviewer 5's assessment that I was expected to achieve 20+ publications and achieve an H-index[23] of 20 was clearly inconsistent with the expectations communicated at the Bush School. These expectations were more aligned with highly ranked doctoral-level political science programs. Few of the full professors in my Department of Public Service had met that criterion before they were promoted to full professor.

Potential Violations of University Policies

Texas A&M policies stated that *"if possible, do not include more than one letter from the same institution"* and not to use reviewers *"whose objectivity is open to challenge."* One can question whether this simple guidance was followed. The following facts can help provide an answer.

- Reviewers 2, 4, and 5 were former Bush School or Texas A&M employees who worked directly with the department head, and/or other faculty members on the CPC and DPC.

Chapter 3: The Contamination

- Reviewers 5 was a co-author with Dr. Ramsdel, the DPC chair, and was the editor of a book to which the CPC chair contributed as recently as one year prior to my promotion application.

- Reviewer 6 was a co-author with a CPC member.

- Reviewers 3 and 4 worked in the same department at the University of Georgia, contradicting university guidelines against double-stacking reviewers from the same institution.

- Reviewers 5 and 6 worked in the same department at American University, contradicting university guidelines against double-stacking reviewers from the same institution.

- Reviewers 3, 4, and 5 had previously worked together as colleagues at the University of Georgia and were residing in the same general area at the time they submitted their evaluations of my application. Reviewer 5, an emeritus faculty member from American University, had returned to live in the region near the University of Georgia.[24]

So, despite hundreds of full professors within my academic areas being eligible to participate in my promotion process, the department selected reviewers who coincidentally shared affiliations, authorship, and/or employment with our own departmental faculty and/or the same two institutions. Even more striking is the fact that all three reviewers who recommended against my promotion application were living in close proximity to one another, near the University of Georgia. Perhaps these facts were the reason for Dr. Ramsdel's confidence that he had selected reviewers he knew *would not let him down*. Under pressure to explain the official rationale for some of these facts, Dr. Ramsdel produced the following internal memo that included his signature only. The names and affiliations of the faculty mentioned are omitted.

Dr. Ramsdel's Memo on the Decision to Reject Dr. Bright's Reviewer Nominations

We did decline to seek outside letters from a number of the people Leonard Bright nominated because they were not qualified by virtue of the institutions where they worked or because their scholarly records would not merit promotion to full professor here or in a comparable program (and both in most cases). Listed below are the people we chose not to invite along with a brief explanation for that decision.

<u>Dr. Bright's List</u>	<u>Explanation for Rejection</u>
White, male, full professor	He is not at a peer institution, nor is he someone whose scholarly record would qualify him for tenure at Texas A&M, much less for a position as a full professor. His research seems to consist almost entirely of government reports as opposed to books or articles in refereed journals.
White, female, full professor	Her college is not a peer institution, nor does it have a public affairs program that is highly regarded. Although she does have a scholarly record, it is not probably not that would merit promotion to full professor at Texas A&M.
Black, male, full professor	He is the dean of a good school of public affairs. He is an active scholar but does not have a strong record in terms of the quality of his publications. I don't think we would consider him as a full professor here. This was a close, judgment call on my part. We could have asked him to write a letter, although his accomplishments as a scholar were not comparable to those of almost all the people who agreed to serve as external reviewers.

Chapter 3: The Contamination

Black, male, full professor	*He is not at a peer institution and he does not have the publication record of a full professor at a research institution.*
White, male full professor	*His university is not a peer institution, and he does not have the publication record of a full professor at a tier-one research institution.*
Asian, male, full professor	*He is not at a peer institution. He is an active scholar but does not have the publication record of a full professor at a tier-one research institution.*
White, female, full professor	*Her university is not a peer institution. She has moved around a lot, and it appears as if she is currently at ... Although she is a very active scholar, the Bush School faculty took a dim view of the quality and placement of her work when she interviewed for a position here a number of years ago. I did not think her assessment of Professor Bright's work would be valued for that reason.*

This memo was a flagrant insult to the reputations of these highly esteemed members of academia. The fact that these individuals were not invited to participate in my promotion process on personal opinions about whether they worked at a peer institution, were tenurable at the Bush School, the number of universities they worked at, or had prior job interviews at the Bush School were not in any way supported by university policy or department practices. These rejected reviewers were full professors, well respected, active scholars, employed at peer-accredited schools, and some were national academy members. The external reviewers that I proposed were also diverse in terms of gender and ethnicity. Yet, every female and faculty of color included on my list was dismissed out of hand.

Web of Deception

Texas A&M policies gave my department complete power in shaping the most important aspect of my promotion process. There were enough facts to question whether the goal was not to select a group of independent external reviewers who fairly represented the experts in my field. They dismissed most of the reviewers I proposed (all of whom were highly accomplished full professors) and then claimed that they did so because the reviewers *"did not have the appropriate credentials"* to take part. The strongest aspect of my tenure applications in the past was the external reviewers. This was on full display during the concurrent tenure review processes I underwent before I had been hired at Texas A&M years ago. As previously presented, there were comments about how *"remarkable"* and *"unprecedented"* it was that none of the 17 external reviewer letters they received were negative about my research accomplishments. Apparently, they learned from that experience, which may have caused them to use their *special* reviewers on this go-round.

The only reviewer who had no relationship with any of the faculty members in the department was Reviewer 1. Astonishingly, email records showed that Reviewer 1 expressed difficulty in receiving instructions on how to submit his recommendation to the department. I was grateful that Reviewer 1 persisted in following up with the department in writing. Doing so made it difficult for his very positive review of my performance to be discarded. It is not possible to know if the department would have moved my file forward with only five reviewers, the minimum that Texas A&M policies allowed, had Reviewer 1 not persisted in remaining involved.

Certainly, there are many legitimate questions about the solicitation strategy my department used in my promotion process. Did the department's strategy violate, at the very least, the spirit of Texas A&M's promotion policies regarding independence? If so, how would such strategies be justified if uncovered? One possibility centered on the department's request that I provide a list of "favorable" reviewers, under the promise that those names would have been added to their list, while also sharing their list with me, expecting I would include those individuals on mine. Had I agreed, the department could have later selected the reviewers in question and then argued that they had been proposed by me, when they had in fact been provided to me by the department.

Did my refusal to comply with the department's request cause it to seek an alternative route? This would align with its later rejection of most of my proposed reviewers, claims of "difficulty" in finding willing participants, and the sharing of damaging off-the-record information. If this interpretation is accurate, my experience suggests that the external review process is vulnerable to manipulation and in need of reform. Ultimately, it was the responsibility of Texas A&M administrators to safeguard the integrity of this process, and I allege they failed to do so.

CHAPTER 4:

Cooking the Books

My application for promotion was officially underway with the solicitation of the external reviewers. The promotion dossier was complete once the reviewer letters were obtained. This started the internal review process. The process involved the department promotion committee (DPC), department head, college promotion committee (CPC), dean, and the university president, who made the final decision. Each of their recommendations and decisions was expected to be based on the information in my completed promotion dossier. The decisions and recommendations were then captured in deliberation memos that discussed the merits of my accomplishments and included a tally of the votes for or against. Each memo was then added to my promotion dossier and forwarded to the next decision maker for their consideration (see Appendix F for the full deliberation memos).

The two committees (DPC and CPC) were composed of faculty members eligible to vote. At Texas A&M, eligibility was based on the rank of the candidate seeking promotion. Only faculty members who held a rank at or above the rank being sought by the candidate could be involved. Since I was seeking promotion to the rank of full professor, only full professors in the department and college considered my case.

The administrators (i.e., department head, dean, and university president) involved in the process were expected to fully review my completed dossier and consider the recommendations of their respective faculty committees before they made their final decisions. However, the decisions the faculty committees reached were only advisory to the administrators and thus had no binding effect. For example, the DPC issued its recommendations to the department head, who considered the case before issuing the final decision on behalf of the department. Similarly, the CPC considered the department head's decision before issuing its recommendations to the dean, who then issued the final decision on behalf of the college. At Texas A&M, the final decision on promotion was made by the university president.

One important characteristic of the promotion process used at Texas A&M was that I had no formal ability to be involved once my dossier was completed. This differed from the practices of universities that grant candidates full access to the promotion process to respond at each level of the review. Texas A&M's policies only gave candidates the right to be informed of the recommendation at each review level. This prevented me from reviewing the letters and questioning the motives behind the department's process and the reviewers' independence. This guaranteed that the contamination that entered my promotion review through the solicitation process went unchallenged. The conclusions of the DPC, department head, and CPC in my promotion case are reviewed next.

Deliberation Memos, Votes, and Recommendations

The DPC was the first committee to provide its review and recommendations. This committee unanimously voted (0-3) against my application on the grounds that my research fell short of the standards. They argued that my teaching and service were on par. However, they wrote that my research record, which included 14 single-authored journal articles and a book chapter that focused on public service motivation, was *"thin and lacking in high-impact, widely recognized journals for a tier-one research university."* The committee relied heavily on the opinions of three of the reviewers (Reviewers 3, 4, & 5).

Dr. Green, the department head, was next in line to review my application. After she had *"satisfied [herself] that the committee's assessment [was] thorough and objective, and otherwise in accordance with our by-laws and Texas A&M regulations,"* she fully supported the conclusions of the DPC. She added, *"despite [my] strengths in teaching and service, [my] research output did not meet the standards for promotion to full professor at a tier-one research university."* In like fashion, the CPC unanimously supported the recommendations of the DPC and the department head (in a vote of 0-4 against), and then they piled on that my research reflected the accomplishments of a *"mid-level associate professor than a full professor."* The conclusions reached by my department and college all hinged on their assessments of my research accomplishments.

The next stage of the promotion process should have involved the dean of the Bush School (Retired General Mark Welsh). Dean Welsh declined to participate, citing his inability to be "fair and impartial" towards me. In fact, I received no updates from any dean, nor was I ever notified of any dean's decision, which was mandatory in this process. In the next chapter, I will explore what led to his decision.

The Promotion Analysis

It is important to review how my case compared to how previous promotion cases were handled in the department and college. Two professors (Professors Vaughn and Gerber) were promoted to the rank of full professor within a four-year period of when I applied. In fact, they both participated in the deliberation process and voted against my promotion application. To show just how blatant the double standard was, this section will walk through the facts. The promotion policies and goals with respect to teaching, research, and service for all three of us were the same. We were all supposed to be held to the same policies and expectations. I obtained Professor Vaughn and Gerber's complete promotion files and will now compare our research accomplishments and treatment.

Just the Facts

TABLE 2

A Comparison of Gerber, Vaughn, and Bright's Peer-Reviewed Publications, Single Authorships, Total Citations, H-Index, & Highest Journal Impact Metrics

	Gerber	Vaughn	Bright
Number of Peer-Reviewed Publications Since Tenure/Promotion	16	6	8
Percentage of Single-Authored Publications Since Tenure/Promotion	6%	17%	75%
Google Citations Since Tenure	1159	1112	1128
Total Google Scholar Citations	2459	1189	1271
H-Index Overall	23	12	10
Highest Journal Impact Metric	2.718	1.491	2.466

Table 2 compares the facts with respect to single authorship, citations, and other impact metrics for Professors Vaughn, Gerber, and me. This analysis will help establish the benchmarks prior promotion candidates achieved and identify any differences in how those benchmarks were applied in my promotion case. This information showed that Professor Vaughn was promoted to full professor with fewer published works, fewer Google Scholar citations, and a lower journal impact factor than Dr. Gerber and me. Dr. Gerber had a higher H-index and more publications. However, most of her publications were multi-authored, while mine were mostly single-authored. Most notably, even though Professor Gerber had more publications, our top journal impact metrics were nearly identical.

Furthermore, Table 3 provides a comparison of the journal quality for publications by Professors Vaughn, Gerber, and myself. This was important given the focus the promotion committees placed on the journals I published in. Table 3 lists the journal impact factors that were associated with each of our highest cited publications by year of employment at the time of our applications. Again, this information revealed that the journal quality for all three of us was similar.

Examining the Promotion Records

A closer examination of Professors Vaughn and Gerber's records suggests I was treated differently. There are at least four major inconsistencies. First, the DPC's claim that my research record of 8 peer-reviewed papers at Texas A&M within a seven-year period was "thin" and "not typically expected of a candidate for promotion to full professor" contradicted Professor Vaughn's case. He published three peer-reviewed publications, an edited book, and a textbook[25] within an 8-year period at Texas A&M as an associate professor before being granted promotion to full professor. One of the primary justifications that the department used to support its claim

TABLE 3

A Comparison of Gerber, Vaughn, and Bright's Top Citations by Year of Employment (Yr), Number of Citations (Cites), and Journal Impact Metrics (Impact)

Gerber			Vaughn			Bright		
Yr	*Cites*	*Impact*	*Yr*	*Cites*	*Impact*	*Yr*	*Cites*	*Impact*
6	578	NA	3	202	0.529	5	435	2.466
7	247	2.718	2	125	1.491	4	305	2.444
1	178	2.371	2	102	0.529	2	248	2.444
6	146	NLP*	1	88	0.529	6	107	1.364
9	109	1.733	5	81	0.529	7	54	1.364
11	99	2.121	8	38	1.491	8	39	1.364
15	95	NA	4	35	0.120	10	36	1.364
			1	25	0.529	13	11	1.364
			5	21	0.641	12	11	N/A
						4	10	N/A

*No longer published

that Professor Vaughn had achieved national research recognition was his Google Scholar statistics. In fact, the DPC chair wrote that Professor Vaughn's case was:

> *Bolstered by other scholars who are citing his research extensively in their own work, Professor Vaughn's work has now been cited more than a thousand times. This is an impressive total that gives evidence that Professor Vaughn's work is having a significant influence on the research community.*

Interestingly, Dr. Ramsdel, while serving as the interim department head during Professor Vaughn's full promotion process, capped his support and wrote that:

> *I feel that Professor Vaughn's scholarly record does meet the threshold for promotion to full professor... with Dr. Vaughn's citation total exceeding 700 at this point in his career, one can conclude that his work is having an impact on his field.*

Ironically, even though my Google Scholar citation metric exceeded 1300 (nearly twice as high as Dr. Vaughn's metric), there was no definitive statement that my work impacted my field.

Second, the department's *"general-field journal"* expectation was not applied to Professors Vaughn nor Gerber during their promotion cases. In fact, in Professor Vaughn's case, the DPC noted that he had *"access to general [field] journals"* and *"very high-profile outlets,"* and determined that he did not have any publications in any of them. Similarly, many of Dr. Gerber's reviewers argued that most of her peer-reviewed publications were placed in second-tier and sub-field journals, and yet these facts were not held against either of them.

The DPC's determination that I was required to publish in *"highly ranked general-field journals"* was the same argument the department used to support their attempt to withhold tenure from me years earlier. As readers may recall, Dean Crocker and Dr. Hopkins squarely and appropriately dismissed that specific argument based on prior college practices and university promotion policies. Also, the university president (Dr. R. Bowen Loftin) and Board of Regents all agreed with Dean Crocker's recommendations. The reformulation of this argument still did not resolve these problems. The department's promotion guidelines required candidates to publish in *"leading peer-reviewed journals in their substantive field, in the fields of public or international affairs, or in relevant disciplines."* Publishing in general-field journals was not a requirement for promotion at Texas A&M, despite the faculty's continual insistence that it was for me.

Third, Dr. Ramsdel tucked a statement in the DPC memo that *"it was difficult securing external reviewers of Dr. Bright's research."* This statement violated university guidelines, which stated that a *"lack of response from a reviewer who has been asked to send a letter should not be interpreted as a negative statement against the candidate."* However, his comment may have been an attempt to justify violating university promotion policies with respect to the solicitation of the external reviewers. The statement is also consistent with Reviewer 5's advice that the department should state that *'no one is willing to review [my] case'* as a way out of considering my promotion candidacy. Professor Vaughn's promotion memos notably lacked such an assertion. He had six outside reviewers decline involvement, just one fewer than I had.

Fourth, Texas A&M policies emphasized the importance that outside reviewers should be arms-length from the candidates to maintain the integrity of the review process. It would not be difficult to expect that reviewers who are close affiliates, friends, and co-workers of the candidates would be unduly favorable. None of the reviewers used in my case were close professional affiliates of mine at any level. However, the records of both Professor Vaughn and Gerber suggest that this was not enforced in their processes.

For example, two of Professor Vaughn's *"very"* supportive external reviewers admitted they maintained close professional relationships with him. One reviewer mentioned that Professor Vaughn and he had worked together on each other's edited books and also served on governing boards and in leadership roles together. A second reviewer acknowledged he was a former coworker at another college and had even served as a personal reference for Professor Vaughn when he had applied to Texas A&M years earlier. Based on my interpretation of Texas A&M's

promotion policies, neither of these two reviewers should have been allowed to contribute. Instead, the conclusions of these reviewers were broadcast throughout the deliberation memos and used to support the decision-makers' conclusions.

Using reviewers who have some affiliations with the promotion candidates may not have been an outlier. An examination of Professor Gerber's promotion case also revealed that reviewers who had personal and professional affiliations with her were also used. One reviewer acknowledged knowing Professor Gerber for over a decade and had worked closely with her on a state-funded project as the head of a consulting firm. Another reviewer acknowledged knowing her for *"quite some time"* and revealed that they had served together on various advisory committees for federal agencies and on many academic panels.

Examining My Annual and Post-Tenure Reviews

The DPC, department head, and CPC's conclusions contradicted seven years of my performance evaluations. These evaluations consistently communicated that I met department and university research expectations. Table 4 summarizes the annual review conclusions I received from three separate department heads, year-by-year, over a seven-year period.

At no point over a seven-year period did my annual evaluations conclude that my research performance did not meet departmental, college, or university expectations. This trend was furthered during my post-tenure review, which according to university policy:

> *Assessed whether the individual is making a contribution consistent with that expected of a tenured faculty member; provided guidance for continuing and meaningful faculty development; assisted faculty to enhance professional skills and goals; and refocused academic and professional efforts, when appropriate.*

TABLE 4

Year 1-7 Summaries of Annual Reviews

Year 1	Praised my journal outlets and noted that I had a *"very productive year."*
Year 2	Stated that my research was making a "substantial contribution" in my field and summed up that I had a "productive year."
Year 3	Asked that I consider two additional journal outlets and concluded that I had a "successful year."
Year 4	Noted my publications and journal outlets, raised no concerns regarding them, and concluded that I had a "good year."
Year 5	Stated that my research record was "strong," my journal outlets were "important in the field," and that I had a "good year
Year 6	Commented that I "had a most successful and productive year" and that I had "an excellent record of productive scholarly achievement"
Year 7	Praised my research record as a "noteworthy record of productive scholarly achievement" and concluded that I had "another good year."

Both the annual and post-tenure reviews evaluated faculty performance against department and university expectations. One difference was that post-tenure reviews were more comprehensive than annual reviews. Another difference was that my annual reviews were primarily conducted by the department heads with informal input from the senior faculty. However, in post-tenure reviews, the senior department faculty weighed in formally and directly. My post-tenure review committee, composed of all full professors, concluded that my research record *'clearly exceeded the level associated with a satisfactory rating'* (see Appendix G for the Post Tenure Memo).

The conclusions reached in my promotion case were entirely inconsistent with the feedback I received in my annual and post-tenure review evaluations. These evaluations are among the few formal processes that provide faculty with clear, documented performance feedback. Notably, all three full professors who participated in my post-tenure review also served on the committees that reviewed my promotion application just one year later. If they had genuine concerns about my research accomplishments, they had a professional obligation to raise those concerns clearly and consistently well before my promotion case. Yet, none of the deliberation memos from the DPC, department head, or CPC reference the feedback documented in my annual and post-tenure reviews.

The stark discrepancy between the positive assessments openly documented in my annual and post-tenure reviews versus the promotion evaluations presented behind closed doors is deeply concerning. This situation raises fundamental questions about fairness, bias, and consistency in the promotion process. If my annual or post-tenure evaluations had been unfavorable, would these assessments have been directly referenced as reasons for the promotion decision?

Few would disagree that performance evaluations should be consistent and fair. My case raises numerous questions. Is it unreasonable to expect faculty members to have noticed obvious problems with the characteristics of the external reviewers, the treatment of other promotion candidates, and the inconsistencies with prior assessments? How prevalent is the use of close friends, allies, and associates in academic promotion processes? Some research suggests that these characteristics are increasingly prevalent and problematic.[26] These problems should have set off all kinds of alarm bells. Academic leaders must answer why their alarms went silent.

CHAPTER 5

The Defense

My complaints about discrimination were dismissed by Texas A&M. University leaders took every opportunity to deny vehemently that anything wrong had occurred, even with the evidence in their possession. Now that they had their reports, investigations, and individuals involved all singing the same song, they went on the offensive to redirect attention from the problems I uncovered. This strategy took at least two forms.

Their Needs Improvement Plan

The first strategy in their attempt to redirect attention away from the serious allegations I raised centered on a new determination that my performance was poor and now in need of improvement. Dr. Green told me after the department recommended denying my promotion that I was *"two years away"* from being ready. Later in the conversation, she followed this up with a request that I withdraw my application. When I refused, she stated that my decision would be a mistake. Consistent with this threat, Dr. Green attempted to re-characterize my work in a much poorer light during my very next annual performance evaluation. Despite being within her first year as department head, she determined that my current and past research accomplishments were poor and in dire need of improvement to put a nail in my coffin. She then proposed a formal performance improvement plan supposedly intended to correct my research performance. I was warned that refusing to cooperate could cause my dismissal.

Not only did I refuse to cooperate in Dr. Green's improvement plan, but I also immediately filed an internal grievance. I disputed her assessment, arguing it was baseless because it did not align with the standards outlined in the department's bylaws, as required by university policy. She also failed to explain why her new conclusions contradicted the precedent set by the Bush School in all previous annual reviews over seven years. I won this grievance. Dr. Green's annual evaluation was rescinded by the university, and the needs improvement plan was tanked.

The Dean's Recusal

The second strategy in their attempt to redirect attention away from the serious allegations I raised centered on the college dean's recusal from my promotion process. Around the same time the department head informed me of her needs improvement plan, Dean Welsh informed me that he was recusing himself from my promotion and that another dean had been asked to review my file. He wrote that his decision was in my *"best interest"*. I doubted that a dean from a different college could provide an accurate review of my accomplishments. I was also curious as to why his recusal was purportedly in my best interest. When I asked Welsh to formally give his reasons for making such a move, he refused to do so, especially in writing. I learned later that he had already announced his plans to withdraw to OREC investigators months earlier. His continued involvement in my affairs puzzled me. How could Dean Welsh perform his duties regarding me in other areas when he was deserting his post in my promotion process?

Dean Welsh's formal declaration of recusal from the process, and his refusal to explain why in writing, raised many concerns for me. I wondered if he held some unexplained biases that would affect my future at Texas A&M. So, I emailed the DOF asking that an alternative dean be provided for all evaluative matters concerning me. In response to my email, I received the following from Dean Welsh.

Emails between Dr. Bright and Dean Welsh about the Decision to Recuse

Dean Welsh	*The only thing I have recused myself from is the dean's review of your promotion dossier, because I believed that was in your best interest. I will consider your concerns about the annual evaluation (the needs-improvement plan) in a timely way.*
Professor Bright	*Please specifically address how withdrawing from something as important as my full professor promotion process is in my best interest, and why it is now in my best interest for you to judge other similar cases involving me? You cannot simply turn on and turn off that kind of decision. Your declaration effectively means that you are biased.*
Dean Welsh	*Dr. Bright, your note to me alleges that Dr. Green didn't follow the proper process. I'll review department, college, and university guidance and get back to you.*
Professor Bright	*Dean Welsh, you did not answer my question. I asked that I be provided the formal reasons that Texas A&M accepted for why you declared*

Chapter 5: The Defense

> *yourself a conflict of interest which you say is in my best interest.*

I followed up this exchange with the following message to the DOF and to the provost.

Email to Provost about Dean Welsh's Recusal

> *Dear Provost,*
>
> *In the interest of fairness to me, I have asked Dean Welsh to address why his recusal during my promotion process was "in my best interest." I believe the reasons (e.g., conflict of interest) for his recusal have greatly influenced not only my promotion process, but also will negatively influence other future evaluative actions regarding me. Therefore, I formally request that my question be addressed.*

A month later, Dean Welsh, accompanied by the university ombudsman at Welsh's request, agreed to meet with me in person to explain his rationale for his recusal decision. After this meeting, I sent the following message to the provost, expressing my concerns with Dean Welsh's explanations.

Dr. Bright's Email to Provost Requesting an Alternate Dean

> *Dear Provost,*
>
> *Today I met with Dean Welsh to hear why he recused himself from my full promotion process, since he would not give his reasons in writing. According to Dean Welsh, he recused himself because of the actions I took by notifying him and the university of the cheating, discrimination, and retaliation that were present in my full promotion process. He repeatedly described my rightful actions to have the university address these irregularities and offenses as aggressive, angry, and emotional because I was receiving a "no vote" from the faculty. Accordingly, this angered him and prevented him from making an unbiased decision.*

> *In response to my request that he support an alternative dean for all of my future evaluative actions given his admitted bias, he stated that it would not be fair to give the less important yearly responsibilities of evaluating me to another dean. However, when I asked if he would recuse himself again if I decided to reapply for promotion, he stated that he was unsure but would consider recusing himself again. This is unacceptable. Biases cannot be turned on and off as Dean Welsh is attempting to do.*

> *Ultimately, Dean Welsh caused irreparable injury to my full professor promotion when he suddenly abandoned his responsibilities as my dean for a non-emergency and very flimsy reason. Based on his explanations, I am now even more concerned that he holds a substantiated bias. If he was unable to judge my promotion then because of his stated bias, I do not trust that he is able to be a fair judge now and in the future. So once again I am requesting an alternative dean for all evaluative matters concerning me.*

Dean Welsh's refusal to cooperate in my promotion appeared to be because of his anger over my efforts to have my discrimination, retaliation, and workplace hostility allegations investigated, particularly by the EEOC. His response to my question about whether he would recuse himself again should I decide to reapply for promotion in the future was disturbing. He stated that his decision would be based on his *"approval"* of my *"behavior"* in the future. This was a classic D.A.R.V.O (Deny, Attack, Reverse Victim and Offender) strategy. In this tactic, perpetrators of harm deny their actions, attack the person confronting them, and then portray themselves as the true victim. Coined by psychologist Jennifer Freyd, the concept highlights how abusers deflect accountability and distort narratives to maintain power.[27] I was not moved by this retired general's military-style attempt to label my rightful request for an investigation as unruly on my part.

Chapter 5: The Defense

Some may ask, would it not be reasonable for someone with an admitted bias to remove himself from my promotion process, to not to injure it? My answer is yes. However, the dean's actions seemed suspicious. He removed himself from my promotion but fought to stay involved in other matters. He should have recused himself from my promotion and any other evaluation if he truly wanted to protect me.

The University President's Decision

Nine months beyond the normal promotion schedule, I received this message: *"President Michael Young denied your application for promotion to Professor"*. Later, in an affidavit, Young gave the following justification:

> *My decision against promotion to full professor was based upon my independent review of Dr. Bright's submitted materials. This review led me to conclude that Dr. Bright's scholarship did not yet merit promotion to full professor.*

A narrative was constructed suggesting my promotion issues arose from my failure to meet standards and my conduct. Of course, I refused to accept this narrative and fought against it. I saw these efforts as a sign that Texas A&M's support of a discrimination-free workplace was a declaration of war. It was a war against anyone who challenged their narrative. Regardless of the evidence I emphasized, the university leaders pushed full steam ahead to redirect attention from the concerns I raised and re-characterized me as undeserving of promotion. This may have been enough to make some people withdraw complaints or seek new employment. I, however, did neither. Running from the problem would not solve the problem. Also, based on my experiences at UofL, I knew similar problems were in every workplace. I was incapable of outrunning them. My only real option was to stand and fight back, which I did. My persistence reached the University Grievance Committee, which looked at my complaints.

The University Grievance Committee

The University Grievance Committee (UGC) was a standing committee of faculty elected from each college or school within Texas A&M. It was one of the most prominent faculty bodies that addressed unresolved complaints between the faculty member, their department, college, and/or university administrators. The Texas A&M grievance policies stated:

> *The UGC will have the right to decide whether the grievance merits a detailed investigation by the UGC. Submission of a petition will not automatically entail investigation or detailed consideration thereof, in determining whether to proceed.*
>
> *If the UGC determines that a detailed investigation is justified, the petitioner will be provided with an opportunity to present his or her case. The UGC may interview any witness they deem appropriate to the investigation and request documentation from the grievant, respondent or a third party pertinent to the case.*
>
> *The UGC hearing subcommittee shall recommend to the Dean of Faculties through the chair of the UGC an appropriate course of action. The Dean of Faculties shall forward the UGC recommendation to the Provost, together with his or her recommendations.*
>
> *All UGC hearings and subcommittee hearings will be recorded. The hearing shall be closed unless the faculty member requests otherwise.*

Despite the key role the UGC served for faculty and for the university, the final decisions reached by the committee had no binding effect on the university's future decisions. The university does not disclose how often it accepts the UGC's conclusions. However, I would surmise that the committee had no assurance that its decision would be accepted by university leaders. The real power of the UGC was the symbolism of a recommendation reached by a representative body of faculty, experts, and peers.

Quickly, I submitted my complaint to the UGC, and it agreed to investigate my case. The committee organized a hearing to ask key questions that guided their inquiry. I asked that the investigation into my complaints be open to the public. This was a crucial decision as it gave me the opportunity to get video recordings of the hearings and interviews conducted with the parties involved in my case. I gave an opening statement to the UGC that placed my experiences at Texas A&M in context (see Appendix H for my UGC opening statement).

Interview with the Dean

After my address to the UGC, the committee conducted video-recorded interviews with several principal parties and fact witnesses to my complaints. Two of the interviews were with Dean Welsh and Dr. Ramsdel. While I obtained Welsh's interview, the university refused to release the interview conducted with Dr. Ramsdel. Now, the dean had already gone on record with OREC investigators a year earlier regarding many of the same questions the UGC would investigate. However, the UGC probe was different in terms of the skill and composition of the committee members. The UGC, unlike the OREC investigation, comprised experienced professors. The OREC investigation involved inexperienced, newly minted lawyers. These differences would have a profound effect on how my complaints were investigated. Members of the UGC asked various questions that probed the dean's perceptions about discrimination, Dr. Ramsdel's involvement, my treatment in the Bush School, as well as the facts about my experiences. While this chapter does not explore the hearing in its entirety, I have dedicated a YouTube account to examining the hearing.[28] The discussion below will focus on several noteworthy lines of questioning. Again, these exchanges were edited for clarity.

Disparate Impact and the Experiences of Black Faculty

One line of questioning focused on the unique experiences of Black faculty members in the promotion process at predominantly white educational institutions.

UGC Chair   *So, I was wondering, in both the promotion's situation and the annual review, to what extent did the department and/or you consider things that might have disproportionate or disparate impact? So, there might be standards that look like they are reasonable, but in fact may not be reasonable when applied to people of different circumstances.*

Dean Welsh   *Yeah, I think. I think you always have to be concerned about that, but I think Dr. Green is a new department head, and we are we talking about the annual review, now?*

UGC Chair   *Both the annual review and the promotion.*

Dean Welsh   *OK?*

UGC Chair   *For example, in the annual review the discussion about the impact factor of the journals.*

Dean Welsh   *I have not seen the entire promotion dossier. As soon as the provost started the investigation based on Dr. Bright's email to her, she terminated or stalled the promotion process. She suspended it and started an investigation. The dossier had not yet come to me. It was in my other office. I had never seen it. I still have not seen it. So, all I have seen were the reports from both the DPC and CPC. And that's what I've seen, and I saw the final notice notifying us that President Young had concurred with the package's recommendation to not*

> *promote. At the time, the DPC letter that they forwarded made sense to me, and I understood the logic behind it. Now, I'm not a scholar. I freely admit that, so I rely on my senior academic leaders here. You need to understand that.*
>
> *And so, when the DPC committee says that they are not concerned about the quality of work, they're not worried about his ability to be a full professor. I have never heard a negative comment about Leonard Bright in terms of being a hardworking, competent professor ever. I've never heard a negative comment about him. The question was just maybe not yet. Maybe the research portfolio needs to be a little bit stronger. That's essentially what the DPC committee said. The department head had the same view, and the CPC had the same recommendation.*
>
> *All of them were unanimous votes, so I felt there was a strong feeling among the scholars in the college that he had not met the hurdle to become a full professor. There was no discussion that he couldn't meet the hurdle or that he wouldn't eventually meet the hurdle, just not yet.*

Cunningly, Dean Welsh side-stepped the committee's questions about disparate treatment. Later, the committee would readdress this issue from another angle.

Inconsistencies in the Annual Review

The second question explored the contradiction between my obligations and the DPC and CPC's reasons for their negative recommendation.

> UGC Chair *So, just to follow up. The one thing that was interesting in the annual review documents that we saw was his time effort. His effort was characterized as 60% for teaching, 30% for research, 10% for service. When somebody's*

> *commitment to a particular aspect of academic life is a minor commitment, 30% is not the majority, how does that become the dominant driving force for promotion?*

Dean Welsh   *I think the issue is more did he meet the standard that the department has set up for promotion to full professor. I think there was an attempt to be as honest as possible in the process, which is a good thing. There has been a renewed emphasis on research in the Bush School over the last two years. Well, there's been a lot of discussion about it. We stood up a research committee and enabled them. They never had one before. We tried hard to follow the university's guidance on this. There's been a lot of discussion in the departments about research being a renewed focus area, and I think that all of that just led to the point where they just didn't think his research portfolio in general was quite ready.*

UGC Chair   *Even though it was a 30% commitment?*

Dean Welsh   *Even with a 30% commitment, which is not unusual in the social sciences, at least. I encourage you to talk to Dr. Green about that when you meet with her. She can give you exactly the reason behind setting that.*

UGC Chair   *So, to your knowledge, were the external reviewers instructed that Dr. Bright's research commitment was 30% and his teaching was 60%?*

Dean Welsh   *I don't know the answer to that question. I'm sorry, I don't know.*

This was an important question because it spoke to the expectations delivered to the external reviewers. These expectations can influence how reviewers interpret the performance records of candidates up for promotion. The fact was that my research commitment was contracted as only 30% of my work responsibilities, which was a minority stake when compared to my teaching and service responsibilities. However, the reviewers were not provided with this information. They most likely assumed research consumed most of my commitment, like it is in most departments at research tier-one universities.

Shifting Performance Standards

A third line of questioning centered on the shifting performance standards in the department. The committee questioned the dean's suggestion that promotion standards were raised.

> UGC Member 4 — *So back to some clarification for what you were just talking about. I hear you mentioned that in the last two years the school has been trying to move to a more research-oriented sort of place. However, my experience across different universities is that if you're hired under a particular paradigm or a particular way or culture or expectation, when it is time for you to go up for promotion, whether tenure or promotion to full, it's very hard for someone to shift mid-career. If he was hired and then in just the last two years, there's a shift in the school, does he now have to rebuild his whole career? It sounds like you would then expect someone to meet expectations that have recently ramped-up in your school, when it takes us, as scholars, to build these portfolios over 5, 6, and 7 years. So, I'm trying to understand. Could you speak more about this transition and how you guys have a plan for people who were hired under, a different sort of protocol or a different level of expectation as far as scholarship is concerned.*

Dean Welsh	*Yeah, I don't think there was any overt... I don't think anybody would say back when Leonard was hired there wasn't a focus on research. But my point was that the Department has really focused on it over the last couple of years, and so has the college. I think that back then, I don't remember the years, but if you look at the annual reviews included in the pack of material you were sent, there was some mention back in Year 3 or so by Dr. Ramsdel. One of those reviews telling Dr. Bright, look, as a suggestion, you might want to look at publishing in different types of journals, so it's not the first time it's been mentioned. It wasn't a consistent point made over time clearly in his annual reviews. I don't know what was said in conversation within the office over the years between then and now, I don't know.* *I do know that Professor Hopkins, who was the previous department head, I know Dr. Bright has put in writing that he supported him and guided him to go ahead and push forward for promotion. That's not Dr. Hopkins' recollection. Professor Hopkins told me when we were looking into this, he actually, before he left, he told him, well, not yet. You know, you probably got a year to keep working on it. Get some more materials together and make sure that it's a no-brainer. That's his recollection. He doesn't remember ever telling him, OK, it's time to go pushed it this year. So, I don't know what was discussed with Leonard year to year. Clearly, one of the things we should learn out of this and have been talking about here is direct*

Chapter 5: The Defense

> *communication really matters. Very honest feedback really matters.*
>
> *Uh, and I think that's an issue, not just here. I think it's an issue, probably in many colleges and around the University, but we've got to be better about providing feedback and in annual reviews and feedback in post-tenure reviews every time we have a chance to sit with a faculty member, we ought to be telling them where they stand and where they stand relative to where they're trying to go. It's not just are you performing acceptably as an associate professor, but are you on track for full? And if not, why not? And is that what you're looking for? And so that's the conversation I've been having with our department heads here and one we have to keep having and we certainly learned that from this situation.*

UGC Member 1   *If I can just say something. I'm very glad to hear that you feel that you have to learn that direct communication is important, but I'm just wondering why Dr. Bright should be the casualty of your department's learning experience?*

UGC Member 4   *Yeah.*

Dean Welsh   *I don't. I don't know that Dr. Bright is the casualty of it because I don't know.*

UGC Member 1   *You haven't yet established that he's not, Sir.*

Dean Welsh   *What? Well, no, but I mean, well... I don't know that he is.*

The tenure and promotion standards used at the Bush School had not changed since they were created years before my arrival in the department. Dean Welsh tried to deflect from the two faculty members who were promoted to full professor with similar and lower performance accomplishments than mine. He wanted the UGC to accept that the department's research standards had been raised conveniently just after Dr. Vaughn and Dr. Gerber were both promoted to full professor. Similarly, Dean Welsh's mischaracterization of my annual review was telling. He pointed to a suggestion in one of my annual reviews that I *"consider"* two general-field journals for my future publications, but then disingenuously failed the mention that (in that same file) his predecessor (Dean Ryan Crocker) directly dismissed this very argument because it was inconsistent with department and college promotion standards and past practices.

The Dean's Recusal Rationale

A fourth line of questioning focused on Dean Welsh's reasons for withdrawing from my promotion. They also looked at how this differed from his continued involvement in other evaluations of me.

UGC Member 2   *You touched on it again moments ago. You said that you didn't recuse yourself from the process because you were angry with him, but because of..., I think you said, his behavior and communication style.*

Dean Welsh   *Yeah.*

UGC Member 2   *Can you explain what it was about his behavior and communication style?*

Dean Welsh   *Yes sir, two things. One was, if you have a conversation with Dr. Bright, there is a*

Chapter 5: The Defense

narrative behind his concerns. Everything from his initial allegations, the subsequent grievances, and complaints, whenever you talk to him, whatever the conversation was, when it comes out the other end, in his words, it supports his grievance.

The second thing is that his communication with people during this entire now almost 16-month process has been aggressive, not civil, almost bullying in some cases in terms of communication style. Uh, and I told Dr. Bright in our meeting that I was just disappointed in that when I considered that this was someone who is trying to become a full professor in our college. I believe that civility and respect for others is really important, especially when we're in a school that teaches us that in terms of public service and serving the breadth of citizens you'll be dealing with when you leave here. So that was my concern. I come from a culture where that is really an issue. So direct communication is really encouraged in the United States military.

I was disappointed in his behavior, and I really questioned whether he was ready just yet. If this was the way he was going to respond when things didn't go his way and he would adopt this style of communicating with others. Did that, should that affect his ability to be a full professor? And because I felt I was too close to the problem because the college that I'm happened to be leading was still under the EEOC investigation, as far as I knew at that time, I felt it was the fairest thing to Dr. Bright to recuse myself and let

> *someone who had none of that potential baggage take a look at his file and do a pure assessment of how is he doing in terms of teaching, research and service.*
>
> *This was not an easy decision. It would have been much easier to do it myself, but I was afraid that I already knew what the answer was going to be because of the way I felt at the time.*

So, according to Dean Welsh, he recused himself to do me a favor! He argued that his decision would not be based on my performance, because my *"behavior"* was supposedly so bad, but provided no proof of such. This made no sense at all! Later during the hearing, he escalated his narrative, stating that I was a *"bully, uncivil,* as well as *unfit for public service."* Once again, this narrative was one of Dean Welsh's go-to strategies to redirect attention from my concerns about my treatment in the promotion process.

Few would disagree that a manager's job is to cope with all employees, even those whom they may deem as difficult because they filed an EEOC complaint. In most organizations, it is never acceptable for a manager to recuse themselves from any part of their work for the reasons provided by Dean Welsh. Unless there is a conflict of interest, managers are expected to do their jobs. Given Welsh's claim that he was not an impartial judge, I worked to have him removed from every evaluative matter that involved me. If he had an admitted bias that would injure my promotion process, then his bias would injure other processes that concern me. Inexplicably, Welsh fought against being reassigned. The committee also questioned him about this oxymoron.

Chapter 5: The Defense

UGC Member 2 — *Why later on when he had a second grievance, pertaining to the department head, why did you feel then you could reasonably stay involved?*

Dean Welsh — *Yeah, that's a fair question. I thought they were based on facts. They were based on interpreting policy, looking at documentation that has been presented, looking at the justification behind a particular assignment and deciding was it fair or not. Yeah, I don't see a need to defer that. I don't hold grudges. I don't get angry at people I worked with before. I never have. I've got a long track record and a lot of people you can talk to about that. I don't do that and so this was a matter of still being in the immediacy of the moment with still an EEOC investigation ongoing involving the Bush School. It just didn't feel appropriate for me to be the person making that decision. Right or wrong, that was my logic.*

Dean Welsh was trapped. He could not explain away his attempt to defend his decision to remain involved in my evaluations after revealing that he had a bias against me. If he held the best intentions for me at heart, he would have recused himself from every evaluative matter concerning me. To me, Welsh's selective recusal might have been a strategic maneuver. It allowed him to avoid making a final, appealable decision on the tainted promotion, while still maintaining control over my career in less scrutinized areas like annual reviews.

The Blame-Shifting Game

The committee seemed to have a tough time believing Dean Welsh, especially his statements about my behavior being a legitimate reason for his recusal. Their frustration with his explanations became noticeable. As the hearing continued, Dean

Welsh seemed to realize that his responses were not convincing. As he worked harder to sell and justify his actions, the committee expressed more skepticism and disbelief.

UGC Member 4   *I have one more question. I heard you use the words, People want him to have over the top, and so I've heard sort of subjective things like that. Do you think it's possible that if he were better liked people could have interpreted things differently? It really sounds like people wanted to not have any conflicts with him, so to speak. So, they may have said, oh, you should have a few more things, but for so many people I know that go up two years later, the few more things they end up having, it's not that different. So, I just... I don't know... I just hear something underneath this where, subjectively speaking, I wonder if he were better liked by his peers, they would have done differently.*

And again, nothing, I'm not really hearing anything. The language is very interesting. I just wanted to note that it's very interesting. It seems like if he were not as abrasive by other's interpretations, perhaps people would have been more supportive, and that's the problem.

Dean Welsh   *Yeah, I would agree with that. I don't think that people didn't like Dr. Bright. It could have been true on an individual basis, but I've been here for four years. I have never heard people talk negatively about him. He is the guy who comes to work, to go to work. He works hard. He's here all the time. He does his job. There's never been an issue of that.*

At this point in the hearing, Dean Welsh's explanations about my *"behavior"* unraveled. He said I was a bully, uncivil, and unfit for

Chapter 5: The Defense

public service. He then contradicted himself by saying everyone liked me and he'd never heard negative comments about me. Several members of the committee pressed him on this contradiction as the conversation continued.

UGC Member 4 — *So how could someone get that feedback and then expect to not get promoted? That just seems so... You can understand his confusion, right?*

Dean Welsh — *That's, that's a great question. I... I think yeah. They don't understand how he didn't understand. I wasn't in the conversations. I can't tell you.*

UGC Member 1 — *Could it be bias then? I'm sorry, if he was so well liked, he did his work so well... I mean, what is the one thing that supports the negative review? I mean, why would people do that then?*

Dean Welsh — *I think..., well, he wanted to push his promotion package in, and I think when it got considered the criticism has been of his research outlets. That's the big thing. It's not anything else.*

UGC Member 2 — *No, earlier you said he was aggressive, he didn't behave, he didn't behave in a civil manner, and he bullied people.*

Dean Welsh — *This is after the fact. This is... I... I never saw that before from Dr. Bright. This is not a daily problem. I don't know if he does it to other people. But when he got news that he didn't like, his reaction was noticeable in the way he communicated to people. So, that's what bothered me and why I recused because I think that's a very significant component. Everybody doesn't have to agree with me. But to be a full professor, I believe,*

> *in a college you should be civil. You should be a respectful and respected colleague. You should be able to deal with people when things aren't going well in a manner that shows respect and civility.*

UGC Chair   *Dean, I am troubled by that characterization. This may be, in a sense, goes to the heart of how people perceive differences in behaviors where the behaviors are racist or not, and one of the troublesome things in our own country has been the characterization of African Americans, who are seeking specific outcomes, as aggressive and bullying and not respectful. You know, there is a language that is associated with the history of racism. I'm not saying that you are racist, but what I'm saying is that there might be triggers that get pulled where somebody's perceived, if they're aggressive about wanting certain outcomes, as more inappropriate. I am just putting that out there.*

Welsh's whiplash was stunning. In one breath, I was a model professor, and in the next, a bully. He could not provide satisfactory answers to the real problems of discrimination, retaliation, and other problems that I uncovered in my promotion process. Many of the answers he gave appeared contradictory. He claimed I did not follow faculty advice against seeking promotion. Under questioning, he confessed that some faculty members had told him they had never informed me of the advice. He argued I did not do enough to be promoted, despite my performance being similar and/or higher than the last two promoted faculty. Many of the important complaints that I raised regarding the promotion process were unaddressed by Dean Welsh: Why the department used four external reviewers (of the six used in my case) who were employed at the same two departments and universities; why half of the external reviewers were former co-workers of the Bush School; why the department use their co-authors as reviewers; why most of my proposed reviewers were dismissed; why all three reviewers who recommended against promotion previously worked together at the University of Georgia and were residing in the same geographic area at the time of their evaluations; and why a faculty member with a documented history of hostility against me chaired the process?

Even worse, upon providing no convincing explanation for his actions or those of his faculty, Dean Welsh escalated and resorted to a tried-and-true tool: character assassination.[29] It was a clear demonstration of how quickly praise could turn to character assassination when he and the institution felt threatened. The history of character assassination of Black males in America is deeply entwined with systemic racism and cultural narratives that have long portrayed us as inherently problematic. Alford A. Young Jr., in his seminal work *"Are Black Men Doomed?"*, explores how society has constructed and sustained a damning image of Black men as incorrigibly dangerous and morally deficient.[30] This portrayal has persisted and shaped public perception and policy. Young argued that this narrative not only marginalizes Black men but also silences our voices, denying us agency in defining our own identities and futures. In his article for the National Academy of Medicine, Young further examines how these portrayals contribute to social unworthiness, leading to exclusion from fair treatment in institutions like education, employment, and healthcare. Hence, character assassination is not merely symbolic, but has real consequences for how Black males are treated, understood, and supported in society.[31]

Interestingly, this was not the first time that Mark Welsh oversaw subordinates who were involved in a scandal. In 2014, as the Chief of Staff of the U.S. Air Force, General Welsh had to address a cheating scandal that engulfed the U.S. Air Force's nuclear command.[32] An investigation revealed dozens of officers responsible for operating intercontinental ballistic missiles had been cheating on proficiency exams. These officers were sharing answers to proficiency tests, which compromised the integrity of the examination process. This raised serious concerns about the readiness and reliability of the personnel tasked with overseeing the nation's nuclear arsenal. The scandal led to the removal of several high-ranking officers, with some facing disciplinary action ranging from reprimands to court-martial proceedings. Eventually, Mark Welsh went on record stating that *"cheating or tolerating others who cheat runs counter to everything we believe in as a service. People at every level will be held accountable if and where appropriate."* It was unfortunate that these basic principles were not fully applied in my case under Mark Welsh's leadership as the dean of the Bush School. The Air Force cheating incident (among other scandals) prompted widespread scrutiny of Mark Welsh's leadership approach.[33]

While I believe that Dean Welsh's behavior was motivated by the personal animosity he held against me for the actions I took to expose the problems I discovered in my promotion process, there may be other reasons worth considering. Was Dean Welsh's behavior driven by a misguided sense of loyalty to his faculty, a crippling fear of litigation, or pure ambition? There is no definitive answer. Welsh was not a career academic, had not achieved a doctorate, had very little (if any) work experience in civilian academic institutions, and was essentially learning on the job as Dean at a major research-intensive institution. This could have been one reason he made the mistakes that he made. He could have been motivated by ambition to ascend to the position of university president. In fact, Texas A&M has a fondness for military leaders, especially since it was originally founded as a military school in 1876 and still has strong ties with the military to this very day. Welsh would not be the first general to serve as Texas A&M University president. Welsh was also well positioned to follow the same path as Dr. Robert Gates, one of the Bush School's past deans, who was selected as Texas A&M's 18th president. These reasons may have motivated him to distance himself from the problems that I was exposing in the most extreme way he could. In fact, Dean Welsh was a finalist for the university presidency after Michael Young resigned, but he was declined in favor of Dr. Katherine Banks, who became the 26th president.

CHAPTER 6

The New Beginning

I repeatedly alleged that my promotion process contradicted the principles of a fair and independent review, and it was inconsistent with Texas A&M's written promotion policies. I discovered that my promotion process was hijacked by a group of faculty members who I alleged rigged my promotion to fail. Despite the mountains of evidence that I presented, university leaders refuted my concerns and aggressively defended the actions they took against me. Thankfully, the UGC took my allegations seriously and investigated them thoroughly.

A few weeks after my appeal, the UGC concluded its investigation and issued its final report to the Dean of Faculties (DOF). The DOF oversaw the promotion process, supposedly to ensure that its policies and procedures were followed. It was general practice for the UGC's final report to be forwarded to all parties involved in the grievance investigation, including the faculty member who started the grievance. This practice was consistent with university rules that stated that faculty members are entitled under Texas law to access their personnel files. However, in a complete break with normal protocol, Texas A&M withheld the final UGC report from me. I made multiple requests to the DOF, provost, and president offices for a copy of the report. Unbelievably, my requests were met with silence or a statement that I *"already received it."*

The Provost's Grievance Decision

The provost issued the following decision:

Email from the Provost about UGC Investigation

> *I have received and reviewed the report of the UGC, as well as the supporting documentation for these grievances.*
>
> *Therefore, I find that the evaluation process for the promotion of Dr. Bright did not violate university guidelines and criteria. Furthermore, I concur that Dean Welsh should be recused from any future decision regarding Dr. Bright and that an alternate dean be appointed to oversee any personnel or supervisory actions.*
>
> *My decision on this matter is final and these cases are closed.*

In sum, Texas A&M denied my application for full promotion, withheld the UGC's report from me, and then exonerated the actions they took against me in my promotion process. These decisions were inconsistent with the evidence that I had gathered and contradicted the university's professed commitment to the Aggie Code.[34]

Continued Retaliation in my Evaluations and Salary

The provost's statement that my case was closed did not resolve or close the matter for me. I continued to face retaliatory actions from my college, especially in my annual evaluations and merit salary determinations. A few years after I defeated Dr. Green's attempt to mis-characterize my research as needing improvement, I discovered that she and the dean had also approved a significant across-the-board salary increase for every associate professor in the department, except me. I argued that their decision was another act of retaliation for my EEOC complaint and efforts to seek fair treatment in my promotion process. I was forced to file another annual review and salary disparity grievance to address the issue.

At Texas A&M, salary and annual review grievances are first heard by the department and then the college, before the DOF makes the final decision. In like fashion, the department head and dean both recommended against my grievance on the grounds that nothing was wrong. Dr. Green and Dean Welsh argued that my compensation aligned with that of my colleagues, noting that the professors who received salary increases were subject to heightened external pressure within the field of economics. Fortunately, a new interim DOF was appointed. He decided to commission an ad hoc committee to conduct a formal salary analysis to look closely at the issue (see Appendix I for the committee's full report).

The ad hoc committee, composed of three tenured faculty (from across the university), found serious inconsistencies and concerns in the Bush School's assessment of my salary, particularly relating to comparisons with colleagues. One argument that Dean Welsh advanced was that I was now suddenly a *"political science"* faculty, and that my salary exceeded that of other political scientists at Texas A&M. This was a highly disingenuous statement. Not only was the political science department not a department in the Bush School, nothing in my contracts, scholarship, experience, nor education supported their argument that I was a political scientist! The committee correctly noted that I was not a political scientist and should be compared with similar scholars within my department. Their analysis showed that my salary was only marginally higher than less experienced colleagues, but lower than what my experience, performance, and impact warranted.

The committee's examination of economist salaries revealed further inconsistencies. They questioned the rationale behind higher salaries for economists, noting the uneven application of salary adjustments within and across the two departments within the Bush School. Some economists received substantial raises regardless of external hiring pressures, while others did not, suggesting a lack of equity in salary decisions.

The committee also criticized the PSAA Department's annual evaluation process, highlighting inconsistencies in how my research was judged. Positive evaluations in some years were contrasted by later assessments questioning the impact of my publications, despite citation data indicating significant scholarly influence. The committee found the scoring system used by Dr. Green was unclear and inconsistently applied, with me receiving dramatically different research scores despite being highly cited.

In conclusion, the committee found merit in my complaint, identifying salary discrepancies and inconsistent evaluations that did not withstand scrutiny for *"equity, merit, or consistency."* After receiving the committee's report, the interim DOF accepted their findings. He concluded his report (see Appendix J) with the following statement.

DOF Memo about Dr. Bright Salary Equity Raise

I recommend that Dr. Bright's salary be adjusted upwards to recognize his time in rank and consistent productivity across the years. Both elements should be sufficient to justify moving him into the range of the three economics faculty in his department while still honoring the principle of developing and supporting a discipline-based salary structure (all three have less time in rank and cumulative productivity is lower or comparable).

I won. When I received and read these reports, I was thankful for the courage and leadership of the committee members and interim DOF. I continued to press forward.

The Aftermath of Welsh's Removal as my Dean

The provost's decision to remove Dean Welsh's supervisory responsibilities led to a merry-go-round of alternative deans, where I had the *pleasure* of being assigned three different alternative deans over two years. It quickly became clear that the alternative deans were unwilling to fully embrace a role that put them in direct conflict with one of their peers, especially one that many believed was possibly an heir to the university presidency. Even a signed memorandum of understanding that spelled out the responsibilities of the alternative dean was not enough to ensure that I was fairly treated. Two years later, the last alternative dean I was assigned revealed that he was given assurances from the provost that he would not have to follow the tenets of the agreement he signed. When I refused to allow him to alter the terms of the agreement unilaterally, I was given an ultimatum by the new interim provost. I was told to accept the new terms of the agreement or be reassigned back to Mark Welsh. I refused to accept the new terms as dictated, and as a result, they reassigned me back to Dean Welsh. However, I continued to fight back against my treatment and the coverup at Texas A&M in at least three different ways.

Lawsuit against Texas A&M

One of the first actions I took to continue my fight against my treatment was to sue in Texas State Court. I sued for discrimination, retaliation, and against Texas A&M's failure to follow its established promotion rules. Once again, I considered the impact that this decision would have on my future at the university and on my career. I accepted the fact that I might face more retaliation and discrimination in the future because of my decision to sue. I also understood that my career advancement might be stalled, and my reputation blacklisted. However, the decision not to fight for myself was not an option that

Chapter 6: The New Beginning

I considered. As I already knew, leaving Texas A&M would not solve these problems.

Unfortunately, this was the second university where I had experienced workplace discrimination and a hostile work environment. The problems that I faced at Texas A&M may be present everywhere in the academy, especially when academic leaders fail to do their jobs effectively.[35] A search for greener pastures would only allow my experiences to go unchallenged. I stayed, stood my ground, and fought back. Even though I accepted the fact that my lawsuit might not prevail, it was important that Texas A&M be held accountable for its promotion processes and written policies. I wanted to have my case heard by an impartial outside party. Predictably, to escape accountability, Texas A&M invoked a *"plea to the jurisdiction"* motion. This plea is typically made by major public universities, which are purportedly immune to most legal complaints. Texas A&M lawyers argued that the university has *"academic determination:"* a term created to shield effectively against external scrutiny, no matter how flawed the promotion process I underwent.

After two years, the 272 District Court Judge agreed with Texas A&M's motion, dismissed my case with prejudice, and thus blocked my ability to have my day in court. I appealed this decision to the Tenth Court of Appeals, which upheld the lower court's decision. Certainly, I was disappointed with the outcome of my lawsuit. I wanted to have my day in front of a jury of my peers, but the deck was stacked against me, especially in a state like Texas. It is nearly impossible for cases such as mine to proceed forward in such forums. Courts have become the home-field advantage for many public institutions, like Texas A&M, which have political connections, resources, and special legal loopholes to maneuver skillfully in this environment. Outcomes like this cause some to question seriously whether some courts are systems of justice, or arenas for legal gymnastics.

Nonetheless, the legal outcomes of my lawsuit did not dampen my resolve.

My Second Promotion Application

Four years after my initial application, I submitted my case for promotion to full professor for a second time. This was the second action I took to continue my fight against my treatment. During the intervening years, I remained productive in terms of my research, teaching, and service. Remarkably, I observed three other professors (each with fewer years of experience and fewer accomplishments) quietly advance to full professor, secure endowed chairs, and receive generous research support. Not once did the department or college extend encouragement for me to reapply, not even as a gesture of goodwill. I could have applied sooner, since the university gave me the option to reapply two years after my initial submission. However, I did not for a couple reasons. For one, it took time for me to learn what happened. The EEOC, grievance hearings, and lawsuits were long processes that required patience on my part. When I felt confident that I got as much information as I could and clearly understood what had happened in my promotion process, I moved forward.

Next, I seriously considered not reapplying. After many days and nights of discussions with my wife Christina, I thought better of it. Christina was adamant that they had been caught. She believed they could not continue to withhold the promotion easily or quietly. I knew that very few black professors gain full professorships, and it was crucial that I not give in to any feelings of doubt about my chances. I had a responsibility given the documented challenges that Black professors experience in attaining promotion, particularly to full professor. So, I recommitted to refusing to let the toxic work environment erode my hope for advancement. Steadfastly, I remained committed to the goal, sustained by my faith and my sense of purpose.

Chapter 6: The New Beginning

As soon as Mark Welsh was reassigned to me as dean, I immediately reapplied. I resubmitted my second promotion application with a few differences. This time I insisted that Dr. Ramsdel be disqualified from serving as the chair of my promotion process, though he still participated as a member of the DPC committee. I also submitted only a group of external reviewers who were faculty of color and highly accomplished. My goal was to stop the department from repeating its strategy of excluding the women and faculty of color from my list of external reviewers. Last, I sent direct email communications to the new university president, Dr. Banks, the new vice president of Faculty Affairs,[36] and to Dean Welsh reminding them of what happened during my first application for promotion.

Interestingly, while I was not given details of the internal deliberation letters or the external reviewers they used, there were a few noteworthy differences this time around. First of all, I receive all required notifications at each level of the review process. One after the other, I was notified that each level voted unanimously in favor of promotion, except for one "no" vote from a member on the DPC committee. Unlike his decision during my first promotion application, Dean Mark Welsh did not recuse himself and instead recommended affirmatively for my promotion. Importantly, while my publications and Google Scholar citations remained high, I still chose not to publish in either of the two general-field journals that the department attempted to require only of me. In the end, Dr. Banks, the university president, approved my promotion. I finally achieved what I had already earned years earlier, though I had to be twice as good as some of my colleagues.

Summer Storm of Controversy

The third action that I took to continue my fight against my treatment was my decision to go public with my experiences. This opportunity came during one hot Texas summer. During a staged public signing event, amid cheers and celebrations, university officials announced that Dr. Kathleen McElroy had been selected to lead a new journalism program at Texas A&M. Not long afterwards, a storm of media outlets reported that the finalization of her contract was being abruptly stalled and watered down in response to political pressure from a right-wing conservative group's protest of her hiring. Email records revealed that university officials reduced Dr. McElroy's initial job offer from a multi-year directorship, which included the rank of full professor with tenure, to a one-year directorship without tenure. Behind the scenes, university officials criticized Dr. McElroy's ability to achieve tenure at Texas A&M, even though she was a nationally accomplished journalist and a tenured full professor at the University of Texas in Austin. Dr. McElroy, in an interview with the New York Times, expressed that she believed the difficulty she experienced from Texas A&M were *"due to her race and possibly gender."* This controversy contributed to the resignation of Dr. Katherine Banks and the quick appointment of Dean Welsh as the university president, without a national search.[37]

I saw clear links between Dr. McElroy's treatment in the promotion process and my own. Her very public story versus my private story both exposed the behind-the-scenes ways that Black faculty were treated at Texas A&M in the tenure and promotion process by academic leaders. We were both black faculty who were told that we did not deserve to be tenured or promoted, despite our performance and how others were treated. We were both subjected to behind-the-scenes insults that gaslit our existence as members of academia. Her courage in exposing her treatment to the larger academic community inspired me to do the same. So, I wrote an open letter to the university community (see Appendix K) and issued public testimony during a faculty senate meeting. I drew links between my treatment and Dr. McElroy's experiences, and I expressed disappointment in Dean

Chapter 6: The New Beginning

Welsh's leadership. I also asserted that the university was engaged in a cover-up by withholding the UGC's final investigation report, which I believed detailed the problems that existed under Dean Welsh's leadership. Shortly after this meeting, I received letters of support from colleagues across the university. I was also contacted by several local, state, and national news outlets for interviews. My story appeared in the Chronicle of Higher Education[38] and the Washington Post.[39] Then, to my great surprise, I anonymously received a draft copy of the UGC's investigation report.

The UGC Report

With a draft copy of the UGC's report in hand, I saw why the university went to great lengths to keep it from me. The UGC's report was an indictment of the faculty and academic leaders who failed my promotion process. Shockingly, the report also revealed that a senior DOF administrator attempted to justify Dean Welsh's statements that I was a *bully, aggressive, and unfit for public service* using my physical appearance. This official stated I was a *"large individual,"* implying my physical size was threatening. I was stunned by this revelation. The UGC rightfully chastised both Dean Welsh and the DOF for evoking *"awful and damaging Jim Crow-era stereotypes."* Ultimately, the UGC issued multiple findings that confirmed and supported all my allegations. It also detailed the university's failure to follow established rules and policies. They investigated my concerns thoughtfully, resisted the temptation to ignore the truth, and reached fair and reasonable conclusions. The problem was that this was not the final report, but only a draft copy. I was uncertain whether the draft copy had been changed before it was completed.

In a dramatic turn of events, I obtained the final official copy through an open records request by a conservative Texas-based news outlet. I was the subject of an open records request by the

Texas Scorecard.[40] The outlet requested copies of my employment file, course syllabi, and email communications. Upon receiving the notification, I announced I welcomed their investigation into my support of diversity, equity, and inclusion (DEI) programs at Texas A&M. I was completely supportive of the accurate reporting of every email I have written, and documents produced by the university and my fight against racial discrimination and retaliation. I then challenged the Texas Scorecard to get the UGC's final report that Texas A&M refused to provide to me despite my repeated requests. The outlet responded, and the final report was forwarded to me by the university prior to its delivery to the outlet. The UGC's final report in its entirety is available in Appendix L. Below, I summarize the UGC's findings and conclusions.

Summary of UGC Investigation Findings and Conclusions

The UGC issued the following conclusions:

> *Dr. Ramsdel's failure to recuse himself likely tainted the promotion process due to the appearance of conflicts of interest.*
>
> *The process was flawed, with potential contamination from conflicts of interest and biases. The lack of flexibility and inappropriate referee selection likely disadvantaged Dr. Bright.*
>
> *While Dean Welsh's recusal was correct, the reasons he cited reflect problematic biases.*
>
> *Dr. Bright's claims of discrimination were justified.*
>
> *Dr. Bright should be entitled to a fair review for promotion by following the guidelines of the department strictly and by ensuring that members solicited to write the report are impartial and at armslength with each other as required by the guidelines.*

At last, I felt a sense of vindication. My allegations were confirmed. The university wanted me to believe that my concerns and complaints were baseless. They wanted me to feel isolated, hoping I would stop speaking out and/or leave my job. The sheer volume of institutional pushback was meant to be demoralizing. I was encouraged that the members of the UGC saw through these efforts. I appreciated the attention and level of detail they gave to my case and the courage they displayed by speaking truth to power. Unfortunately, to this very day, I am not aware of any action the university took regarding the UGC's recommendations. Despite all the evidence that the university had in its possession, Dr. Ramsdel retired honorably as an emeritus professor, Dr. Green remained in her position as department head, and Dean Mark Welsh became university president. It was just another day in academia-land.

The Ousting of Mark Welsh as Texas A&M President

In an unexpected development two years after Mark Welsh's appointment as university president, his tenure ended after a combination of external political pressures and internal discontent with how he managed another controversy that hit Texas A&M University. Welsh dismissed Dr. Melissa McCoul, an English department instructor who had been secretly recorded by a student objecting to her lesson on gender theories on religious grounds.[41] Welsh initially demoted department leadership before ultimately firing Dr. McCoul after political pressure from the Texas governor and other state-level political leaders. His actions triggered widespread criticism from faculty, students, and academic freedom advocates, especially given his unequivocal pronouncement (just two years earlier) that he would defend academic freedom with *"every breath"*.[42]

Facing mounting backlash from all sides, Welsh stepped down from his position.[43] Advocates of academic freedom argued that Welsh's actions suggested a clear disregard of the rights of faculty and sent a chilling message to the entire academic community.[44] This situation was another painful example of Welsh's failure as an academic leader to support and defend academic values. Perhaps his tendency to sacrifice these values for the sake of expediency, career advancement, or self-preservation ultimately contributed to his downfall.

EPILOGUE

The tenure and promotion process is never fully transparent, rarely openly disclosed, but always presented as objective, neutral and fair.[45] This book provided a firsthand account of my experience in the full promotion process at Texas A&M. It pulled back the veil to show the promotion process I underwent, how performance management problems took root, and how university leaders failed to address them effectively. These are rare and compelling concerns that faculty of all races, genders, and fields can experience in their careers.[46] This case is unique because it discussed my experiences using my actual performance records, which allowed readers to come to their own conclusions. It also adds to the very limited body of empirical research on the experiences of faculty in the full professor promotion process. There are several important lessons university leaders and faculty should learn from this case.

Performance Management Problems are Vast

First, the reasons for performance management problems are vast. To this very day, the only faculty members to have suffered the denial of tenure or promotion in my department (and possibly the entire Bush School)[47] have been women and one black faculty member (me). So, I cannot ignore the fact that my race may have been a major reason for the actions that my department took against me. The UGC report highlighted the influence of race and discrimination on my promotion case, and I fully agree with their assessment. Dean Welsh's repeated accusations that I was aggressive, and the DOF's explanation that I was a *"large individual"* to minimize Welsh's statement were indeed awful.

In fact, I am the only Black faculty member in the history of the Bush School to seek promotion to the full professor rank, as of the writing of this case. This is consistent with the National Center for Educational Statistics, which revealed that black faculty represented only 3% of all full professors in post-secondary education positions. The statistics were even bleaker when the ranking of the university was considered. At Texas A&M, tenured Black professors only represented 3.2% in 2018 and declined to 2.8% of the tenured faculty in 2024.[48] Similarly, Table 5 displays the Chronicle of Higher Education's 2022 percentages of full-time Black faculty members by each NCAA Southeastern Conference (SEC) school.[49] This data suggest that Texas A&M has one of the lowest percentages among SEC schools on average and lags its SEC peers in recruiting and attracting Black faculty. These statistics also underscore the existing research that has consistently shown that the experiences of faculty members of color in academic settings were routinely hostile and difficult.[50]

Yet, problems as insidious as racism or racial discrimination are not the only reasons that can motivate misbehavior in academic settings. Again, there is a strong belief in some corners of academia that the faculty should have the power to choose who works alongside them for whatever reasons they see fit. In my case, years earlier when the department faculty appeared to learn of the problems I had experienced at UofL, I believe some tried to abort a job offer by recommending that I not receive tenure. The faculty's recommendations were soundly rejected by the dean in place at that time. Understandably, some faculty

TABLE 5

NCAA Southeastern Conference Schools Ranked by Total Percentage of Full-time Black Faculty[51] in 2022

School	Percentage
University of Mississippi	7.0
University of South Carolina, Columbia	6.2
University of Alabama, Tuscaloosa	6.0
University of Georgia	5.3
University of Tennessee, Knoxville	5.1
Vanderbilt University	5.0
University of Kentucky	4.8
Louisiana State University, Baton Rouge	4.5
Auburn University	4.4
Mississippi State University	4.4
University of Florida	4.3
University of Missouri, Columbia	4.3
University of Texas, Austin	4.3
Texas A&M University, College Station	3.5
University of Arkansas, Fayetteville	3.3
University of Oklahoma, Norman	2.9
Average	4.71

members may have felt dissatisfied with this rejection, causing them to resent me more.

Similarly, the leadership opportunities I received may have also contributed. I can only imagine how some faculty members felt to watch someone they attempted to drive away receive not only tenure and promotion, but also attractive administrative titles that most would never receive. I am sure they were infuriated! These faculty members may have seized the opportunity to use the promotion process to settle an old score.

The Roots of Performance Management Problems

Second, performance management problems can take root in any aspect of the promotion process. I have argued that they were seeded during my hiring process, infected the committee deliberation decisions, and defended by university leaders after it was discovered. A major contribution of this case study is that it provided the first known account of how these problems can be cultivated in the external reviewer solicitation process. External reviewer feedback is highly influential in the success or failure of promotion candidates. A uniformly positive set of external reviewers will almost guarantee the success of the promotion application, whereas a negative set of reviewers will most likely ensure its failure. So, it is odd that more has not been done to study and protect this incredibly important feature.

Most, if not all, universities typically have policies that attempt to protect the independence of external reviewers. At Texas A&M, external reviewers were to be an *"arm's length"* from the candidate. However, this policy did much less to address the undue bias that stemmed from the relationships that the department faculty had with the reviewers they used. Consider how external reviewers were solicited at Texas A&M. Department faculty had the sole power to decide who to invite to conduct a review. They engaged in multiple private conversations with potential external reviewers and then selected those they believed would provide the feedback they wanted. I seriously doubt that any of the reviewers misunderstood Dr. Ramsdel's intentions during those private conversations. He openly gloated that he had selected a group of reviewers he '*knew and would not let them down.*' This leads me to the next point.

Complicit External Reviewers

Third, performance management problems can be facilitated by the external reviewers themselves. This was one of the most difficult revelations for me to accept. External reviewers should be independent of what the department thinks or desires. They should be selected based on their expertise. To maintain independence and neutrality, the department should not tip its hand and announce its position on the case during the solicitation process. If the reviewers' assessments are not convincing, the department can disagree with them.

Certainly, it is natural for some reviewers to want to know if the department supports the candidate's efforts, and the department may be equally interested in knowing if the reviewer supports its perspective. However, if the process gives in to these inclinations, the entire promotion process will be placed at risk. If the department's support is lacking, some reviewers may refuse to participate. Such decisions are not based on the merits of the candidates' accomplishments, but on a belief that few incentives exist that justify spending hours, days, and even weeks on an assessment that is dead on arrival. The desire to provide a review that helped what they believed were my department's goals appeared strong for at least a couple of reviewers in my case. They showed a willingness to revise their assessments to accommodate the department's wishes. Yet, the absence of any sign of opposition to these practices from any of the reviewers captured on record suggests that this practice may be normalized in academia.

Ambiguous Performance Goals and Policies

Fourth, performance management problems can be aided by vague performance goals and policies. Faculty members have long complained about the lack of clear guidance and consistency regarding the actual benchmarks for career advancement.[52] The academic literature is filled with complaints from not only junior faculty members working toward tenure and promotion,[53] but also from associate professors seeking promotion to the full professor rank.[54] The problem is that ambiguity is an accepted feature of the academic workplace. As a result, some academic settings rely on performance criteria, which specify *how* decisions will be made and the features of performance that will be considered, rather than on *actual* performance goals. Still, one must keep in mind that performance criteria are not performance goals. In many academic settings, the achievement of performance goals is determined through an open debate on a case-by-case basis. This is a problematic characteristic of academic performance management.

While Texas A&M provided an extensive list of performance criteria, there was little clarity as to the performance goals that were to be achieved. The university produced annual, tenure, and promotion policies that highlighted the importance of peer-reviewed research, leading journals, and journal citations. Yet, there was no clarity regarding which journals were leading, the minimum number of publications expected, the minimum number of citations required, and so forth. Interpreting ambiguous performance goals and policies was intentionally left to each faculty to decide for themselves. Even when the department provided clear annual review and post-tenure assessments that determined that I met these unnamed expectations yearly, these decisions had no bearing on the recommendations reached in the promotion process. This situation ensured that any perspective, no matter how inconsistent, could be justified. It opened the door to personnel decisions being driven by emotions, favoritism, and discrimination.

Next, performance feedback should be clear, unambiguous, and relevant. For example, in Birkman v City of New York, a class action lawsuit involving 80 women, a judge ruled that a test that involved carrying a 120-pound dummy on one shoulder up and down a flight of stairs, scaling an eight-foot-high wall and running one mile had little relationship to the qualities needed to perform well as a firefighter.[55] These requirements disqualified women in a field dominated by men. An analogous situation has been occurring in academia. The promotion process has been honed to disqualify faculty members who are not supported, and some academic leaders are doing little to correct this situation.

The Weaponization of Collegiality

Fifth, multistage evaluation processes offer little protection against performance management problems. Faculty decisions are heavily influenced by the norms of collegiality and consensus. Professors are socialized to value group deliberations and seek consensus in decision making. Unanimity is a tool used by academics to communicate that the group stands together on an issue, and that there is no other plausible alternative to their decision that was not considered. Unanimity can send a powerful image of fair, thorough, and systematic decision-making outcomes. This image can be further strengthened by multistage evaluation practices, whereby other faculty groups up or down the chain reach the same conclusive decisions.

Similarly, multistage evaluation practices heighten the appearance of thoroughness through a system of checks on the decisions reached at previous levels. It is an excellent preemptive defense against challenges of bias and especially discrimination. Texas A&M was quick to emphasize to the EEOC that its multistage processes were proof that its performance management outcomes were fair and inclusive. How can multiple faculty members, working on multiple committees, and housed at various levels produce discriminatory and unfair outcomes?

During his interview with the UGC, Dean Welsh replied, *"In some world that's possible, but it's not likely."* However, there are at least two reasons that make such conclusions misplaced.

To begin with, biased outcomes are very possible when the emotional bonds among faculty members, the need for conformity, and the fear of dissent are high. In these situations, dominant group members will seek to solidify their decisions by pressuring other members to concede their differing viewpoints as an act of collegiality to achieve unanimous decisions. This phenomenon is also known as groupthink.[56] Some of the worst actions in American history occurred at the hands of groups and mobs.

Even more, the strong value of collegiality can lead faculty on committees to engage in vote trading. This is the practice of faculty members voting in the manner that another faculty member wishes for reciprocal treatment. For example, Faculty A will expect Faculty B to support a case, expecting that Faculty A will return the favor to Faculty B in another case. I would theorize that there is a strong incentive for such activities when groups are composed of faculty members from different departments. For example, the CPC in my case was composed of four faculty members from two departments: two from my department and two from a second department. It is possible that faculty members from my department expected the faculty members from the other department to defer to their judgments on my case because they had a better understanding of the facts and expectations for promotion in our department. In fact, the OREC investigation revealed that at least one faculty member on the CPC, a member of the other department, was prepared to vote in my favor before learning of the opposition to my application from representatives from my department.

Similarly, for all the professed value that universities place on their fair, thorough, and multi-stage evaluation processes, university leaders have ensured that they are not held to the decisions reached from these processes. At Texas A&M, administrators routinely reminded faculty members that the final decision in all evaluative matters was made by the university president and/or board. This makes every deliberation that occurs prior to the president and board's decisions purely advisory and with no binding effect. Even more, there are no internal rules or policies that govern how the university president or board members make their decisions. Two cases at the University of North Carolina (UNC) that involved Dr. Nikole Hannah-Jones, and Texas A&M involving Dr. Kathleen McElroy suggest these decisions are heavily influenced by politics. Both Dr. Hannah-Jones and Dr. McElroy faced significant opposition from conservative groups and politicians during their promotion processes. In both cases, the universities initially refused to grant these respected scholars tenure and/or promotion because of political pressure. Yet, most times, the rationale for these types of decisions was not revealed. This practice effectively gives university leaders the ability to decide in any manner they see fit.

Case in point, President Young explained that his decision against my promotion application was based on his *"independent review"* of my *"submitted materials"*. This statement suggests he acted independently of previous recommendations and even of the assessments of the external reviewers. Yet, it lacks detail about how he reached his conclusion. It may be the case that he recognized the problems with my promotion process and was trying to distance himself. Whatever the reasons, this statement does not show a great deal of confidence in Texas A&M's multi-stage evaluation process. Still, the university's final decision was indeed the president's responsibility. The problem was that President Young was not an expert in my field of research and thus had little academic credibility to decide the merits of my academic accomplishments on his own. No university president is an expert in every field of research. I believe it would have been much more proper for university leaders to have admitted that problems occurred, and remanded the case back to the department and/or college.

Insulated Institutions

Sixth, academic institutions are insulated from accountability for problems found in the promotion process. It was unfortunate to see the sheer number of administrators in my case who appeared to rubber-stamp the flawed promotion process. Their apparent failure to address the clear evidence of wrongdoing was so profound it bordered on unbelievable. One example centered on the Office of Risk, Ethics, and Compliance (OREC). Texas A&M's policies required that the OREC investigate all discrimination allegations. This office was staffed with lawyers who had little to no experience working in academic departments as faculty members. As I explained, its investigations amounted to asking the parties to admit verbally to committing illegal acts of discrimination, with a full understanding of the consequences such an admission would have on their careers. When these rational individuals refused to incriminate themselves, the OREC concluded that my discrimination claims were *"unsubstantiated."*

In most states, universities are required to publish statistics regarding the outcomes of their internal investigations of discrimination, harassment, and retaliation complaints. These statistics reveal that substantive determinations of wrongdoing are exceedingly rare.[57] One potential reason may be that internal university investigation offices are not designed to incriminate their employers. Instead, these offices appear to gather information to defend their employers in court. Here, in my case, the OREC office promised to withhold its final decision until its investigation was completed, while they were secretly collecting information to craft their response against my allegations. When these underhanded efforts were exposed, and I asked if they would withdraw their conclusions until they completed their investigation, they refused.

Some academic settings have leveraged the ambiguity built into their written policies to give wiggle room to defend any practice as they see fit, when it becomes necessary. For example, the use of qualifiers such as *"if possible," "it is recommended,"* or *"should"* to prefix tenure and promotion policies nullified these policies. They are built-in fail-safes against charges of inconsistency and discrimination. Dishonest, biased, or discriminatory behavior can be defended because their policies do not *actually* forbid it. This has created a situation where some faculty members and administrators have no fear of violating the rules. They are confident that the university will defend them. For example, even though Texas A&M policies required that the department should not use reviewers whose *"objectivity"* was *"open to challenge,"* recommended against soliciting *"reviewers from the same institution"*, and encouraged that all communications with external reviewers be conducted in writing, there appeared to be no fear of violating them. My department's decision to use external reviewers who had close professional relationships with several members of the department; were co-authors and former co-workers in the Bush School; and worked at the same two institutions appeared to make no difference to Texas A&M's decision to go full steam ahead in the promotion process. These are *compelling* problems that academic leaders should have clearly addressed.

Large public universities, like Texas A&M, have achieved even further insulation from accountability for performance management problems given their unique position within the American legal system. They are shielded by layers of policy and governmental privilege that make holding them accountable in court a formidable challenge. One of the most significant obstacles to holding public universities accountable in court is the doctrine of sovereign immunity. As state entities, public universities are protected by laws that restrict the ability of individuals to sue them. Sovereign immunity, originally designed to shield governments from frivolous lawsuits, has evolved into a potent defense for universities facing allegations of misconduct and discrimination. Plaintiffs are required to navigate complex statutes that define the narrow circumstances under which a public university can be sued. Even then, the permissible remedies may be limited. Courts frequently defer to the autonomy of educational institutions, especially in matters of faculty governance, academic standards, and internal disciplinary procedures. Institutions like Texas A&M are skillful at capitalizing on their unique legal protections to prevent plaintiffs from having their day in court.

Leadership Matters

Last, all employees (including professors) should strive to uphold the highest standards of integrity. We are accountable not only to the letter of the law but also to its spirit, avoiding even the appearance of impropriety. Yet, the potential for misconduct within organizations is an enduring aspect of human nature. It cannot be entirely eliminated. As James Madison[58] observed, *"If men were angels, no government would be necessary."* When expectations of good conduct fail, it becomes the duty of leaders to step in and correct the situation.

My experience illustrates the critical role leadership played in maintaining integrity within the promotion process. The courage shown by early leaders (Dean Crocker and Dr. Hopkins) in safeguarding the process from inconsistencies set a high standard, one that later leaders failed to uphold. While early leaders resisted the use of promotion standards that conflicted with written policies and prior precedent, their successors appeared to overlook these inconsistencies. The earlier leaders had the courage to say "no" to the faculty, their successors deserted and recused themselves from their oversight responsibilities, leaving me to navigate the situation alone.

The tenure and promotion process has two essential sides: faculty and administration. Faculty members initiate the promotion process and apply their disciplinary expertise to evaluate the merits of each case. Academic leaders, in turn, ensure that established standards and policies are applied fairly and consistently across all faculty, departments, and colleges. When warning signs or misconduct arise in how the faculty conducts its role, it is the duty and responsibility of leaders to intervene effectively. Failure to do so undermines the integrity of the process and sends damaging ripples throughout the university and the broader academic community.

My Advice to Faculty and Academic Leaders

The situation described in this case can happen to anyone who is not supported by their colleagues and governed by academic leaders who fail to protect the process. The *"not supported"* list is simply a group of individuals who do not fit, for whatever the reason, within the expectations of the power players in their department. Regardless of how you arrive on the list, your membership will influence your work environment.

I was placed on the *"not supported"* list at the very start of my employment at Texas A&M University. I was hired, tenured, and promoted against the wishes of a group of faculty members. These faculty members were not convinced that I should have received tenure, even after nearly a decade of high performance and employment as an assistant professor. They wanted me to enter their workplace as a vulnerable, untenured colleague. Yet, their efforts failed because department, college, and university leaders ensured I was treated fairly and consistently. This sparked growing resentment among some of the faculty, who would become a hurdle to my advancement to full professor years later when new academic leaders, sympathetic to their views, assumed power in the department and college. I learned that the academic promotion process, which involved some of the smartest minds, used multiple levels of committees, and was overseen by a cauldron of administrators, can be rotten at its core. Now, the key question is what can be done about this situation?

Know the Rules

Understanding university policies was essential for me as I maneuvered successfully through challenging academic work environments. Learning the rules requires no special skill or ability and can be done by anyone. Within the first few months of my employment, I studied the policies regarding the promotion standards and grievance processes. I sought to understand not only what the written requirements were but also what the policies did not state. The unwritten rules are the crevices where problems will take root. I did not rely on my department or colleagues to tell me what they were. It was important that I knew them myself. Courage was also needed to make quick use of this knowledge anytime things contradicted written policies.

In addition to the formal rules that govern professional life, there are other important workplace survival strategies worth learning. A few of these strategies include developing a documentation plan, recording meetings, summarizing important conversations in writing, and maintaining a healthy skepticism about the intentions of your managers. Some managers are highly skilled at disarming employees and maneuvering them into less-than-ideal situations. The most adept, and often unscrupulous, among them can appear to be acting in your best interest while quietly advancing their own agendas. The consequences of failing to recognize these situations and respond effectively can be severe.

To this day, I remain deeply grateful that my wife accompanied me to the meeting with Dean Welsh and his senior executive dean. Welsh actually resisted scheduling a meeting that included my wife as an observer, but he eventually relented when I stood my ground. My wife had the presence of mind to record the discussion. At that time, I was hesitant to do so myself. I wanted to believe that Welsh was acting in good faith, that all I needed to do was present evidence of wrongdoing and he would do the right thing. I was naïve. Had I walked into that high-stakes meeting and left without any concrete record of what transpired, I would have been defenseless against the narrative he later tried to build against me. Without the crucial evidence my wife captured, I would have faced an uphill battle convincing anyone that Mark Welsh's (a retired four-star general) account of the meeting was false.

Get the Data

Faculty should have access to all records that pertain to their tenure and promotion case, including the records of similarly situated faculty members recently promoted. It is unfortunate that some universities will certainly work to obstruct the release of this information. When this happened to me, the EEOC and similar state-level agencies, as well as open records laws (especially for public institutions) were indispensable partners.

Frequently, the defense some universities will make against allegations of wrongdoing is to provide a reason for their treatment that does not appear to be illegal on the surface. In my case, the OREC investigated whether the faculty and department involved could provide a *"non-discriminatory reason"* for their decisions. When they did verbally, OREC determined my allegations were not substantiated. Their investigation went little further than this. There was no real investigation of whether their statements were true. This is unfortunate because wrongdoing is always accompanied by a reason. It is foolhardy to accept the view that wrongdoers cannot provide misleading answers, pulled from the ether, to explain away their treatment. The only way to address this situation effectively is to go beyond simple answers and gather hard evidence of the truth.

Disrupt Shady Processes

Transparency in the tenure and promotion process should be the norm in academic performance management. Some universities have an open evaluation process, which gives faculty members the right to review and respond to every decision that was made in the review process. For example, institutions such as the University of Louisville (UofL)[59] and the University of Georgia[60] fully allows promotion candidates to read and respond to the recommendations reached at each level of the review. These kinds of open rebuttal processes give faculty members the ability to address any errors in the record and advocate on their own behalf. Unfortunately, Texas A&M used a closed promotion process. After the faculty submitted their lists of potential external reviewers and dossiers, they were closed out of the process entirely, except for periodic updates on the progress of their cases. Under this system, faculty members have no formal access to review deliberation memos nor the external review letters, much less the ability to respond to them.

Closed promotion processes, like those used at Texas A&M, tilts the scale heavily in the university's favor, assumes that department feedback is offered without bias, and can promote feelings of powerlessness, frustration, and stress in the promotion candidates, especially those who feel (and know) that they are being wronged. Under these systems, promotion candidates are placed in the position of sitting ducks awaiting the hatchet to fall. Administrators often promote the view that wrong candidates should wait, remain compliant and quiet, let the process play itself out, and hope that an unfavorable decision will somehow change at the next levels. I did not follow this advice. Because I knew my concerns were legitimate and not frivolous, I used everything appropriate at my disposal to disrupt the promotion processes.

Clarify Ambiguous Standards

The ambiguity that is at the heart of the tenure and promotion process has been a complaint of many junior and mid-career professors. Yet, many academic departments have done little to address the situation. I have argued that this characteristic is purposefully designed to ensure that the faculty is in control of who works alongside them, as well as provide universities with an exit strategy when things go wrong. Performance evaluation policies should be clear. They should specify what is required by one's academic discipline that reflects scholarly effort and achievement.

In addition, there should be unambiguous appeal policies in place. Faculty members should have the right to grieve negative promotion decisions to an independent group of faculty members before the final decision is made by the university president or board. The feedback from this independent body of faculty should be taken seriously. If the process the independent body of faculty used to reach their conclusions is suspect, the president should remand it back with a clear description of the procedural errors that occurred. The president should not, outside of extreme circumstances, seize the opportunity to go it alone and decide the case without providing a thorough account of the rationale for his or her decision.

Overhaul the Promotion Process

The crux of the tenure and promotion process is the selection of an independent and neutral body of expert external reviewers. Promotion cases are often won and lost on the feedback these reviewers provide. My case suggests that conflicts of interest can result not only from the relationships that the candidates have with the reviewers but also from the relationships that the department faculty can have with them as well. My department selected external reviewers they believed would provide the feedback they wanted to have. The faculty members who serve as the external reviewers should uphold the highest level of integrity, avoiding even the appearance of being compromised. They should not inquire about or wade into interdepartmental politics. Any contact with department faculty members should be avoided. They should voluntarily decline involvement when they have (or have had) close relationships with any of the parties involved in the promotion process.

There are universities with strong protections in place. For example, the University of Georgia requires that the *"head of the promotion/tenure unit and other eligible voting faculty in the unit may not contact [external reviewers] about the candidate's promotion and/or tenure review."* UofL goes further and places the solicitation of the external reviewers in the hands of the college, rather than in the department.[61] The candidates also can review the department's proposed list to address any perceptions of bias and ensure that the reviewers proposed match their field of expertise.

Punish Wrongdoing

A faculty member who had a known history of hostility toward me and my wife should not have led my promotion process. The opinions of external reviewers who were not experts in my field should never have been solicited. The external reviewers, who were past coworkers at the Bush School, and coauthors with members of my faculty, should not have been asked to participate. There should have been no effort on the part of the external reviewers to fine-tune their feedback with the wishes of the department faculty. The written promotion rules (as well as the spirit of those rules) should have been enforced. Taken together, these are obvious and persuasive signs of compelling problems. A promotion process and decision that were reached under these characteristics should have been swiftly rejected.

While I support the perspective that the decisions of faculty should be prioritized in the academic performance management process, this does not come with a blank check. Faculty must uphold the core principles of truth, fairness, and integrity. When the faculty fail in their duty to these values, then it is the responsibility of administrators to address the situation effectively. Under no circumstances should administrators defend wrongdoing. In my case, any dean, department head, and/or faculty members involved in creation of these problems should have been reprimanded and re-educated at the very least. While the provost attempted to limit the harm that Dean Welsh had on my career by removing his supervisory authority over me, this decision was short-lived.

Relax, Enjoy Life, and Keep it all in Perspective!

Coping with the stress associated with hostile work environments can be challenging. Such issues often absorb significant time, attention, and energy, potentially impacting one's personal life and family responsibilities. Over time, these factors may reduce workplace effectiveness, contribute to health complications, and increase the risk of serious negative outcomes.[62] I worked hard to keep these problems in proper perspective. I took time to relax and enjoy life outside the workplace. While I enjoy my job, it will never be my greatest source of happiness. That position goes to my faith and family. So, while I may feel isolated in my workplace from time to time, I know I am never alone. By focusing on the big picture, taking breaks, and engaging in fun activities, I was able to then calmly and strategically address the issues I faced.

I have questioned whether I would have done anything differently if I had known what I was going to face. I must acknowledge that there were a few remarkable individuals who alerted me to the struggles that I would face in this profession, especially as a Black man. Still, I thought I would easily outmaneuver any problems I faced based on my willingness to work hard. I have accepted the hard truth that I could not have outrun, outmaneuvered, or outperformed the problems that came when people made their preferences more important than performance, integrity, and accountability. The hostility I endured in academic workplaces was not a figment of my imagination. These were enemy actions that I addressed head-on, with courage, no matter the consequences. American history teaches us that systematic change, especially for our most deeply rooted problems, does not happen without persistence, challenges, and sacrifices. My experiences gave me far more than a promotion could ever give me. I have a purpose and an opportunity to make an impact on my profession. It is peace that is beyond understanding, and I *now* count it all joy!

NOTES

[1] Google AI, "Define Rig 'Em."
[2] AAUP, *Policy Documents*.
[3] Cui et al., "Quantifying Impact of Teamwork."
[4] Gardner et al., "Putting in Your Time."
[5] June, "The Uncertain Path."
[6] NCES, "Characteristics of Postsecondary Faculty."
[7] Perna, "Sex and Race Differences."
[8] Wijesingha et al., "Glass Ceiling or Murky Waters."
[9] Jameel, "Workplace Discrimination Cases."
[10] I later learned that this statement was false. Only three of the reviewers recommended against my promotion to full professor.
[11] Gardner and Blackstone, "Putting in Your Time."
[12] I have dedicated a YouTube Series titled *How They Rigged My Promotion Process: An Inside Look*" to analyzing this meeting on my YouTube page: The Bright Professor.
[13] "Gig 'em" is a trademark of Texas A&M University that encapsulates the ethos, camaraderie, and resilience that is the core of Aggie culture. The phrase originated in the early 1930s, during a highly competitive football game between Texas A&M and TCU. During the game, a beloved Aggie yell leader, Pinky Downs, exhorted his fellow students to rally behind the team with a new cheer. In a moment of inspiration, he raised his thumb and index finger in a gesture resembling a fishhook, shouting, "Gig 'em", Aggies!" The phrase caught on, becoming an emblematic rallying cry for Aggies across generations. Over the decades, "Gig 'em" has transcended its origins as a football chant, permeating every facet of campus life.
[14] See Cagan, "San Francisco Declaration," Fortunato, et al., "Science of Science,"
 Merton, "The Matthew Effect," and Sinatra et al. "Quantifying the Evolution,"
[15] Each letter received was assigned a number from 1 to 6. The number corresponded to the date posted on each review letters received by the

department in ascending order. For example, Reviewer 1 reviewer letter had an earlier date than Reviewer 6.

[16] Schwartz and Schroeder, "External Reviews."

[17] Rhoades-Catanach and Stout, "Current Practices..in Tenure Decisions."

[18] NASPAA or the Network of Schools of Public Policy, Affairs, and Administration is a membership association with over 300 institutional member schools at U.S. and non-U.S. universities that award degrees in public administration, public policy, public affairs, non profit and related fields. NASPAA is the recognized global accreditor of master's degree programs in these fields. The Bush School public service and administration process was NASPAA accredited.

[19] The issue of editors publishing in their own journals has increasingly become a topic of discussion and concern. See Helgesson et al. and Richardson, et al.

[20] Reviewer 6 can also be considered a public management practitioner/scholar, though I was unfamiliar with his research accomplishments.

[21] Reviewer 3's was an outlier. He was also a respected public management scholar who recommended against my promotion.

[22] Texas A&M's tenure and promotion guidelines required a list of the department's peer and aspiring institutions, if other than Association of American Universities (AAU) and the justification for the selection. The department did not provide this information in my promotion dossier files.

[23] The H-index is a metric used to quantify scholar's academic influence in a single number. A researcher has an H-index of "h" if they have published "h" papers, each of which has been cited at least "h" times.

[24] This was based on information provided in Reviewer 5's bio and vita.

[25] According to departmental bylaws, textbooks are classified as teaching accomplishments and are not considered part of a faculty member's research output.

[26] Blank, "The Effects of Double-Blind," Bilespie, "Experience with NIH," and Sandström, "Persistent Nepotism in Peer-Review."

[27] Freyd. "Violations of Power."

[28] Readers interested in a thorough account of the UGC hearing with Dean Welsh can visit "The Bright Professor" YouTube page (https://www.youtube.com/channel/UCX5PHvdxEIwFs7nEdfshLuw).

[29] Young, "Character Assignation of Black Males."

[30] Young, *Are black Men Doomed?*

[31] Young, Ibid.

[32] Cooper, "Cheating Accusations," DOD, "Press Briefing," and Michael, "Missile Officers Caught."

[33] Brook, "Air Force Chief Gives His Service Top Ethics Marks."

[34] A cultural tradition at Texas A&M which states that "An Aggie does not lie, cheat, steal, nor tolerate those who do." The code took shape during the mid-20th century, likely preceded by West Point's honor code in the early 20th century that "A cadet will not lie, cheat, steal, or tolerate those who

do." Both West Point and Texas A&M's codes appear to have emerged in response to academic dishonesty and misconduct.

35 Coates, "Academic Abuse," Gardner and Blackstone, "I Couldn't Wait to Leave," Park and Kang, "Faculty to Faculty Incivility," Pelletier et al., "Toxic Triangle," and Stalcup, *Surviving Toxic Work Environments*.

36 As part of an administrative reorganization plan, the DOF was dismantled and replaced with the Office of Faculty Affairs.

37 Texas A&M, "President Kathy Banks to Retire."

38 Gretzinger, "Texas A&M Tries to Turn the Page."

39 Stripling, "Behind the Lines." https://www.washingtonpost.com/education/2023/09/05/texas-am-university-diversity-sb17/.

40 The Scorecard was often accused of weaponizing open records laws against faculty who supported diversity, equity, and inclusion (DEI) initiatives.

41 Priest, "How a Secret Recording of a Gender Identity."

42 DeMoss, "Texas A&M Interim President Addresses Media."

43 Stripling, "Partisan Fury Got Him a Presidency."

44 AAUP-TAMU, "Response to the Dismissal."

45 Baez, "Race-Related Service and Faculty of Color."

46 Bronstein and Farnsworth, "Gender Differences," Diggs et al, "Smiling Faces and Colored Spaces," Harris et al, *Stories from the Front of the Room*, Kelly and McCann, "Women Faculty of Color," Laden and Hagedorn, "Job Satisfaction among Faculty of Color," Stanley, "Coloring the Academic Landscape," Turner et al., "Faculty of Color in Academe," and Writer and Watson, "Recruitment and Retention."

47 This statement does not refer to the Department of Political Science, which became a member of the Bush School of Government a few years after my experiences discussed in this book.

48 Texas A&M, "By the Numbers."

49 Chronicle of Higher Education, "Race, Ethnicity, and Gender of Full-Time Faculty."

50 Butner, "Coping with the Unexpected."

51 Total full-time faculty members include all staff members whose primary occupation is classified as instruction, research, or public service. This includes those with and without faculty status.

52 Babcock, "Gender Differences," Fox, "Gender and Clarity of Evaluation," Gardner, "Putting in Your Time," Griffin, "Marginalizing Merit," Kulp, "Clear as Mud," and Rabinowitz, "The Associate-Professor Trap."

53 Ibid.

54 Baker, "Charting Your Path to Full," Blackstone et al., "Putting in Your Time," Chambers, "To Be Young, Gifted, and Black," Freeman, "Toward Best Practices," and Perna, "Sex and Race Differences."

55 Berkman v. City of New York, 812 F.2d 52 (2d Cir. 1987).

56 Janis, *Groupthink*.

57 Here are a few examples of recent statistics produced by Cornell:

Notes

(https://titleix.cornell.edu/statistics/2023-2024/), Texas A&M University (https://titleix.tamu.edu/our-stats/) University of Houston (https://uh.edu/equal-opportunity/title-ix-sexual-misconduct/faqs/previous-years-data-2023/), University of Nevada (https://www.unr.edu/civil-rights/reporting-statistics), University of Texas, Austin (https://compliance.utexas.edu/sites/default/files/documents/dia-22-23-annual-report-final-2024.01.31_1.pdf).

[58] Madison, Federalist No. 51.

[59] See section 2.2.I.8 in the 2023 University of Louisville's College of Arts and Science Personnel Policy and Procedures (https://louisville.edu/provost/faculty-personnel/unit/AS%20Personnel%20Policy%20and%20Procedures%20Board%20Approved%2014%20DEC-2023.pdf).

[60] See section 7.B, in the 2023 University of Georgia's Guidelines for Appointment, Promotion, and Tenure of Academic Rank Faculty (https://provost.uga.edu/wp-content/uploads/appointment-promotion-tenure-guidelines-academic-rank-faculty.pdf).

[61] See Section 2.2.I.6 of the University Louisville College of Arts and Science's 2023 Personnel Policy and Procedures.

[62] Haare, "Outcomes of Work," and Kivimäki, "Work Stress."

REFERENCES

American Association of University Professors. *Policy Documents and Reports*. JHU Press, 2015.

Andrews, Martha C, K Michele Kacmar, and Kenneth J Harris. "Got Political Skill? The Impact of Justice on the Importance of Political Skill for Job Performance." *Journal of Applied Psychology* 94, no. 6 (2009): 1427-37.

Babcock, Linda, Maria P Recalde, Lise Vesterlund, and Laurie Weingart. "Gender Differences in Accepting and Receiving Requests for Tasks with Low Promotability." *American Economic Review* 107, no. 3 (2017): 714-47.

Baez, Benjamin. "Race-Related Service and Faculty of Color: Conceptualizing Critical Agency in Academe." *Higher Education* 39, no. 3 (2000): 363 91.

Baker, Vicki L. *Charting Your Path to Full*. Rutgers University Press, 2020.

Bande, Belen, Pilar Fernández-Ferrín, Carmen Otero-Neira, and José Varela. "Impression Management Tactics and Performance Ratings: A Moderated-Mediation Framework." *Journal of Business-to-Business Marketing 24*, no. 1 (2017): 19-34.

Bassett, Debra Lyn. "Recusal and the Supreme Court." *Hastings LJ* 56 (2004): 657-98.

Blackstone, Amy, and Susan K Gardner. "Faculty Agency in Applying for Promotion to Professor." *Journal for the Study of Postsecondary and Tertiary Education* 2 (2017): 59-75.

References

Blank, Rebecca M. "The Effects of Double-Blind Versus Single-Blind Reviewing: Experimental Evidence from the American Economic Review." *The American Economic Review* (1991): 1041-67.

Blass, Fred R., Robyn L. Brouer, Pamela L. Perrewé, and Gerald R. Ferris. "Politics Understanding and Networking Ability as a Function of Mentoring: The Roles of Gender and Race." *Journal of Leadership & Organizational Studies* 14, no. 2 (2007): 93-105.

Blickle, Gerhard, James A Meurs, Ingo Zettler, Jutta Solga, Daniela Noethen, Jochen Kramer, and Gerald R Ferris. "Personality, Political Skill, and Job Performance." *Journal of Vocational Behavior* 72, no. 3 (2008): 377-387.

Bronstein, Phyllis, and Lori Farnsworth. "Gender Differences in Faculty Experiences of Interpersonal Climate and Processes for Advancement." *Research in Higher Education* 39, no. 5 (1998): 557-85.

Brook, Tom. "Air Force Chief Gives His Service Top Ethics Marks." *USA Today*: July 25, 2014. https://www.usatoday.com/story/news/nation/2014/07/25/ethics-sexual-assault-military/13099979/.

Butner, Bonita K., Hansel Burley, and Aretha F. Marbley. "Coping with the Unexpected: Black Faculty at Predominately White Institutions." *Journal of Black Studies* 30, no. 3 (2000): 453-62.

Cagan, Ross. "San Francisco Declaration on Research Assessment." *Dis Model Mech* 6, no 4 (2013): 869-70.

Chambers, Crystal R, and Sydney Freeman Jr. "To Be Young, Gifted, and Black: The Relationship between Age and Race in Earning Full Professorships." *The Review of Higher Education* 43, no. 3 (2020): 811-36.

"Race, Ethnicity, and Gender of Full-Time Faculty Members at 3,300 Institutions." *Chronicle of Higher Education*. June 2, 2025. https://www.chronicle.com/article/race-ethnicity-and-gender-of-full-time-faculty/.

Coates, Tabitha K.L. "Academic Abuse: A Conceptual Framework of the Dimensions of Toxic Culture in Higher Education and the Impact on the Meaning of Work." *Higher Education Quarterly* (2024): 12536.

Cooper, Helene. "Cheating Accusations Among Officers Overseeing Nuclear Arms." *New York Times.* January 16, 2014: https://www.nytimes.com/2014/01/16/us/politics/air-force-suspends-34-at-nuclear-sites-over-test-cheating.html

Croom, Natasha N. "Promotion Beyond Tenure: Unpacking Racism and Sexism in the Experiences of Black Womyn Professors." *The Review of Higher Education* 40, no. 4 (2017): 557-83.

Cui, Haochuan, An Zeng, Ying Fan, and Zengru Di. "Quantifying the Impact of a Teamwork Publication." *Journal of Informetrics* 15, no. 4 (2021): 101217.

Office of U.S. Department of Defense. *Department of Defense Press Briefing on the Status of Air Force Investigations into Allegations of Illegal Drug Possession from the Pentagon.* 01/15/2014. https://www.legistorm.com/stormfeed/view_rss/388199/organization/31751/title/department-of-defense-press-briefing-on-the-status-of-air-force-investigations-into-allegations-of-illegal-drug-possession-from-the-pentagon.html.

DeMoss, Adrienne. "Texas A&M Interim President Addresses Media, Controversies for First Time." *KBTX.* August 2, 2023. https://www.kbtx.com/2023/08/02/texas-am-interim-president-addresses-media-controversies-first-time/.

Diggs, Gregory A, Dorothy F Garrison-Wade, Diane Estrada, and Rene Galindo. "Smiling Faces and Colored Spaces: The Experiences of Faculty of Color Pursing Tenure in the Academy." *The Urban Review* 41 (2009): 312-33.

Edwards, Willie J., and Henry H. Ross. "What Are They Saying? Black Faculty at Predominantly White Institutions of Higher Education." *Journal of Human Behavior in the Social Environment* 28, no. 2 (2018): 142-61.

Equal Employment Opportunity Commission. *Race/Color Discrimination.* August 26, 2021. https://www.eeoc.gov/racecolor-discrimination.

References

Ferris, Gerald R, Darren C Treadway, Robert W Kolodinsky, Wayne A Hochwarter, Charles J Kacmar, Ceasar Douglas, and Dwight D Frink. "Development and Validation of the Political Skill Inventory." *Journal of management* 31, no. 1 (2005): 126-52.

Flaherty, Colleen. "Botched." *Inside Higher Education.* June 6, 2020. https://www.insidehighered.com/news/2020/06/22/two-black-scholars-say-uva-denied-them-tenure-after-belittling-their-work.

Fox, Mary Frank. "Gender and Clarity of Evaluation among Academic Scientists in Research Universities." *Science, Technology, & Human Values* 40, no. 4 (2015): 487-515.

Freeman Jr., Sydney, Ty-Ron M.O. Douglas, and Trista Goodenough. "Toward Best Practices for Promotion to Full Professor Guidelines at Research Universities." *eJournal of Education Policy* 21, no. 2 (2020).

Freyd, Jennifer. "Violations of Power, Adaptive Blindness, and Betrayal Trauma Theory." *Feminism & Psychology,* 7 (1997): 22–32.

Fortunato, Santo, Carl T. Bergstrom, Katy Börner, James A. Evans, Dirk Helbing, Staša Milojević, Alexander M. Petersen et al. "Science of Science." *Science* 359, no. 6379 (2018).

Gardner, Susan, and Amy Blackstone. "Putting in Your Time: Faculty Experiences in the Process of Promotion to Professor." *Innovative Higher Education* 38, no. 5 (2013): 411-25.

Gardner, Susan K. "I Couldn't Wait to Leave the Toxic Environment." A Mixed Methods Study of Women Faculty Satisfaction and Departure from One Research Institution." *NASPA Journal About Women in Higher Education* 5, no. 1 (2012): 71-95.

Gillespie Jr, Gilbert W, Daryl E Chubin, and George M Kurzon. "Experience with NIH Peer Review, Researchers' Cynicism and Desire for Change." *Science, Technology, & Human Values* 10, no. 3 (1985): 44-54.

Google AI. Response to "Rig'em Colloquial Term." *Google.* August 21, 2025.

https://www.google.com/search?q=Rig%27em+colloquial+term&oq=Rig%27em+colloquial+term&gs_lcrp=EgZjaHJvbWUyBggAEEUYOTIHCAEQIRigATIHCAIQIRigATIHCAMQIRigATIHCAQQIRigATIHCAUQIRigATIHCAYQIRirAtIBCjMyNzQzOWowajeoAgCwAgA&sourceid=chrome&ie=UTF-8.

Griffin, Kimberly A, Jessica C Bennett, and Jessica Harris. "Marginalizing Merit?, Gender Differences in Black Faculty D/Discourses on Tenure, Advancement, and Professional Success." *The Review of Higher Education* 36, no. 4 (2013): 489-512.

Griffin, Kimberly A, Meghan J Pifer, Jordan R Humphrey, and Ashley M Hazelwood. "(Re) Defining Departure, Exploring Black Professors' Experiences with and Responses to Racism and Racial Climate." *American Journal of Education* 117, no. 4 (2011): 495-526.

Gretzinger, Erin. "Texas A&M Tries to Turn the Page From its Summer of Scandal: How a 'Top Down' Leadership Culture Weakened Shared Governance, Leaving the Institution Vulnerable." *Chronicle of Higher Education*, September 29, 2023. https://www.chronicle.com/article/texas-a-m-tries-to-turn-the-page-from-its-summer-of-scandal.

Haar, Jarrod M., Marcello Russo, Albert Suñe, and Ariane Ollier-Malaterre. "Outcomes of Work: Life Balance on Job Satisfaction, Life Satisfaction and Mental Health: A Study across Seven Cultures." *Journal of Vocational Behavior* 85, no. 3 (2014): 361-73.

Harris, Michelle, Sherrill L. Sellers, Orly Clerge, and Frederick W. Gooding. *Stories from the Front of the Room, How Higher Education Faculty of Color Overcome Challenges and Thrive in the Academy*. Rowman & Littlefield, 2017.

Helgesson, G., Igor Radun, Jennie Radun, and Gustav Nilsonne. "Editors Publishing in their Own Journals: A Systematic Review Of Prevalence And a Discussion of Normative Aspects." *Learned Publishing*, 35 (2022): 229-40.

Jameel, Maryam. "More and More Workplace Discrimination Cases are Closed Before They're Even Investigated." *The Center for*

Public Integrity, June 14, 2019. https://publicintegrity.org/inequality-poverty-opportunity/workers-rights/workplace-inequities/injustice-at-work/more-and-more-workplace-discrimination-cases-being-closed-before-theyre-even-investigated/.

Janis, Irving Lester. *Groupthink*. Houghton Mifflin Boston, 1983.

June, Audrey. "The Uncertain Path to Full Professor." *Chronicle of Higher Education*, Feburay, 14, 2016. https://www.chronicle.com/article/the-uncertain-path-to-full-professor/.

Kelly, Bridget Turner, and Kristin I McCann. "Women Faculty of Color: Stories Behind the Statistics." *The Urban Review* 46 (2014): 681-702.

Kivimäki, Mika, Jaana Pentti, Jane E. Ferrie, G. David Batty, Solja T. Nyberg, Markus Jokela, Marianna Virtanen, et al. "Work Stress and Risk of Death in Men and Women with and without Cardiometabolic Disease: A Multicohort Study." *The Lancet Diabetes & Endocrinology* 6, no. 9 (2018): 705-13.

Kulp, Amanda M., Amanda Blakewood Pascale, and Lisa Wolf-Wendel. "Clear as Mud: Promotion Clarity by Gender and Bipoc Status across the Associate Professor Lifespan." *Innovative Higher Education* (2022): 73-94.

Laden, Berta Vigil, and Linda Serra Hagedorn. "Job Satisfaction among Faculty of Color in Academe: Individual Survivors or Institutional Transformers?". *New Directions For Institutional Research* 2000, no. 105, (2002): 57-66.

Levi, Lennart. "Occupational Stress: Spice of Life or Kiss of Death?" *American Psychologist 45*, no. 10 (1990), 1142-45.

Liu, Yongmei, Gerald R Ferris, Jun Xu, Barton A Weitz, and Pamela L Perrewé. "When Ingratiation Backfires: The Role of Political Skill in the Ingratiation-Internship Performance Relationship." *Academy of Management Learning & Education* 13, no. 4 (2014): 569-86.

Madison, James. The Federalist No. 51. In The Federalist Papers, edited by Alexander Hamilton, James Madison, and John Jay. New York: New American Library, 1961.

Merton, Robert. "The Matthew Effect in Science." *Science*, 159 (1968): 56-63.

McCullough, Jim. "First Comprehensive Survey of NSF Applicants Focuses on Their Concerns About Proposal Review." *Science, Technology, & Human Values* 14, no. 1 (1989): 78-88.

Michaels, Jim. "Missile Officers Caught Cheating on Exams." *USA Today*, January 16, 2014. https://www.usatoday.com/story/news/nation/2014/01/15/air-force-drug-scandal/4494675/.

National Center for Education Statistics. *Characteristics of Postsecondary Faculty. Condition of Education.* U.S. Department of Education, Institute of Education Sciences. May 31, 2022. https://nces.ed.gov/programs/coe/indicator/csc/postsecondary-faculty.

Park, Eun-Jun, and Hyunwook Kang. "Faculty-to-Faculty Incivility in Nursing Academia: A Qualitative Systematic Review." *Journal of Professional Nursing* 48, (2023): 1-14.

Pelletier, Kathie L, Janet L Kottke, and Barbara W Sirotnik. "The Toxic Triangle in Academia: A Case Analysis of the Emergence and Manifestation of Toxicity in a Public University." *Leadership* 15, no. 4 (2019): 405-32.

Perna, Laura W. "Sex and Race Differences in Faculty Tenure and Promotion." *Research in Higher Education* 42, no. 5 (2001): 541-67.

Priest, Jessica, Nicholas Gutteridge, and Kate McGee. "How A Secret Recording of a Gender Identity Lecture Upended Texas A&M." *The Texas Tribune*. September 19, 2025. https://www.texastribune.org/2025/09/19/texas-a-m-welsh-firing-professor-gender-mccoul/.

Rabinowitz, Paula. "The Associate-Professor Trap." *Chronicle of Higher Education* 67, no. 11 Feburary 5, 2021. https://www.chronicle.com/article/the-associate-professor-trap.

Richardson, Reese, Spencer Hong, Jennifer Byrne, Thomas Stoeger, and Luis Amaral. "The Entities Enabling Scientific Fraud at

Scale are Large, Resilient, and Growing Rapidly." *Proc. Natl. Acad. Sci.* 122, no 32 (2025): e2420092122.

Rhoades-Catanach, Shelley, and David E Stout. "Current Practices in the External Peer Review Process for Promotion and Tenure Decisions." *Journal of Accounting Education* 18, no. 3 (2000): 171-88.

Sandström, Ulf, and Martin Hällsten. "Persistent Nepotism in Peer-Review." *Scientometrics* 74 (2008): 175-89.

Schwartz, Bill, and Richard G. Schroeder. "External Reviews: What Is Being Done?" *Journal of Accounting Education* 15, no. 4 (1997): 531-47.

Sinatra, Roberta, Dashun Wang, Pierre Deville, Chaoming Song, and Albert-László Barabási. "Quantifying the Evolution of Individual Scientific Impact." *Science* 354, no. 6312 (2016): aaf5239.

Stalcup, Apryll M. *Surviving Toxic Work Environments*. Springer, 2013.

Stanley, Christine A. "Coloring the Academic Landscape: Faculty of Color Breaking the Silence in Predominantly White Colleges and Universities." *American Educational Research Journal* 43, no. 4 (2006): 701-36.

Stempel, Jeffrey W. "Rehnquist, Recusal, and Reform." *Brook. L. Rev.* 53 (1987): 589-667.

Stripling, Jack. "Behind the Lines of Texas A&M's Diversity War." *The Washington Post*. September 6, 2023. https://www.washingtonpost.com/education/2023/09/05/texas-am-university-diversity-sb17/.

Stripling, Jack, and Nell Gluckman. "Partisan Fury Got Him a Presidency and Then It Took Him Down." *The Chronicle of Higher Education*. September 19, 2025. https://www.chronicle.com/article/partisan-fury-got-him-a-presidency-and-then-it-took-him-down.

Amercian Association of University Professors. Texas A&M University Chapter. "AAUP-TAMU Response to the Dismissal of Dr. Melissa McCoul." *X*, September, 16, 2025, 8:56am.

https://x.com/TAMU_AAUP/status/1968675468913135851.

Texas A&M University System. "Texas A&M President Kathy Banks to Retire Immediately: Dean Mark Welsh Named Acting President in Wake of Hiring Controversy." *Campus Life*. July 21, 2023. https://stories.tamu.edu/news/2023/07/21/texas-am-president-kathy-banks-to-retire-immediately/.

Texas A&M University. Office of Academic and Business Performance Analytics. "Texas A&M by the Numbers." 2024. https://abpa.tamu.edu/tamu-by-the-numbers/faculty-demographics.

Thompson, Carolyn J, and Eric L Dey. "Pushed to the Margins: Sources of Stress for African American College and University Faculty." The *Journal of Higher Education* 69, no. 3 (1998): 324-45.

Toutkoushian, Robert K. "The Status of Academic Women in the 1990s: No Longer Outsiders, but Not Yet Equals." *The Quarterly Review of Economics and Finance* 39, no. 5 (1999): 679-98.

Turner, Caroline Sotello Viernes, Juan Carlos González, and J Luke Wood. "Faculty of Color in Academe: What 20 Years of Literature Tells Us." *Journal of Diversity in Higher Education* 1, no. 3 (2008): 139-68.

Usborne, David. "Us Air Force Suspend 34 Airman Manning Critical Nuclear Missile Launch Sites after Discovering They Cheated on Proficiency Tests by Text." *Independent*, January 16, 2014. https://www.independent.co.uk/news/world/americas/us-air-force-suspend-34-airman-manning-critical-nuclear-missile-launch-sites-after-discovering-they-cheated-on-proficiency-tests-by-text-9065357.html.

Walker, Jeffery T. "How to Manage the Move from Associate to Full Professor." *Journal of Criminal Justice Education* 27, no. 2 (2016): 255-70.

Wei, Li-Qun, Flora F.T. Chiang, and Long-Zeng Wu. "Developing and Utilizing Network Resources: Roles of Political Skill." Journal of Management Studies 49, no. 2 (2012): 381-402.

References

Wenneras, Christine, and Agnes Wold. "Nepotism and Sexism in Peer-Review." *In Women, Science, and Technology*, (2010): 64-70.

Wijesingha, Rochelle, and Karen Robson. "Glass Ceiling or Murky Waters: The Gendered and Racialized Pathway to Full Professorship in Canada." *Canadian Review of Sociology/Revue canadienne de sociologie* 59, no. 1 (2022): 23-42.

Williams, Brian N, and Sheneka M Williams. "Perceptions of African American Male Junior Faculty on Promotion and Tenure: Implications for Community Building and Social Capital." *Teachers College Record* 108, no. 2 (2006): 287-315.

Writer, Jeanette Haynes and Dwight C Watson. "Recruitment and Retention: An Institutional Imperative Told through the Storied Lenses of Faculty of Color." *Journal of the Professoriate* 10, no. 2 (2019): 23-46.

Wuchty, Stefan, Benjamin F Jones, and Brian Uzzi. "The Increasing Dominance of Teams in Production of Knowledge." *Science 316*, no. 5827 (2007): 1036-39.

Young Jr, Alford A. "The Character Assassination of Black Males: Some Consequences for Research in Public Health." *In Perspectives on Health Equity and Social Determinants of Health*. National Academies Press, 2017.

Are Black Men Doomed? Polity Press, 2018.

APPENDIXES

APPENDIX A

Email from Dr. Bright to Dean Welsh about Dr. Green

From: Dr. Leonard Bright
To: Dean Mark Welsh

Dean Welsh,

Dr. Green gave me an update on the status of my application for promotion to full professor. She indicated that a three-member faculty committee voted against my application (although she did not give me the vote tally), and she stated that 4 out of 6 of my external letters were not supportive. Based on my conversation with her, it is clear that she is unable and unwilling to advocate for my record. The department head's role in this process is to defend on behalf of the candidates they have worked with over the years. Obviously, I have not worked with her as department head given that she has been in the position for one semester. I had discussed with Dr. Hopkins about whether I should pursue full professorship, and he gave me the go-ahead. Now, I am at a disadvantage of not having a department head who oversaw my performance in teaching, research, and service. As a result, I must take this drastic step to advocate for what I have accomplished, with the guidance and support of Dr. Hopkins. Below is my formal response to my conversation with Dr. Green.

First, new, more arduous research standards are being applied to my case that have not been applied to Professor Vaughn, who is a similarly situated faculty member, was promoted to full professor 2 years ago. During our conversation, Dr. Green stated she resonated with a "rule of thumb" assessment offered by one reviewer, who stated that a google scholar H index of 20 and 20+ published works are the standards for full promotion. She then followed this up with an assessment that my scholarly impact was more consistent with the standards for promotion to associate professor rather than to full professor. This insult suggests that I should not have been hired as a tenured associate professor seven years ago when I had fewer accomplishments. The problem is that the new research standards Dr. Green is referencing have never been communicated at the Bush School or applied to other recent full promotion cases at the Bush School, namely Dr. Vaughn and Dr. Gerber.

Second, it is my strong belief that Dr. Ramsdel's involvement (i.e., as chair of the department promotion committee) in the selection of my external reviewers has tainted this process. A few years ago, Dr. Ramsdel was reprimanded by Dean Crocker for dismissing my wife from a faculty appointment after he and I had a dispute over my role as assistant dean. Given our contentious relationship, Dr. Ramsdel's involvement in the critical selection of reviewers is problematic. As a result, it is unacceptable that the Bush School allowed him to create such an imbalanced set of reviewers, with 4 of the six being external reviewers of his choice. I believe he engaged in an old academic practice of "stacking the deck" with outliers who do not reflect the peers of the Bush School and may not be scholars in my field. This is why I have requested redacted copies of the letters. Based on what Dr. Green told me, most of these letters advocated for standards that are more reflective of those found at Ivy League and/or top 10 programs in the field, which the Bush School is not.

Third, Dr. Green demonstrated a woeful lack of understanding of the importance and breadth of my research. She is unaware, unable, and unwilling to advocate for the research program I have conducted. For example, during our conversation she stated that my "education articles were not impactful" and that I should research other topics. I reject any attempt in hindsight to censor my research on the pedagogical and educational dimensions of public service motivation. These national studies were encouraged by my two previous department heads, one of whom was my coauthor and has shed light on the importance of public service motivation among public affairs students. Even more, President George H.W. Bush himself noted that his legacy will be seen in the impact of the educational mission of the Bush School. I find it hard to believe that an academic leader within President Bush's School would suggest that research on this topic is not valuable.

Fourth, Dr. Green suggested that my high service to the School and University was detrimental to my promotion application, a "drain on my research," and a poor use of my time. I strongly reject these characterizations. The agreements I forged with the previous department heads, deans, and provosts regarding my service to the department and university have been seen as an asset and should not have been treated or spoken of negatively in this promotion process by her. However, her statement confirms the warning that I received from Dr. Hopkins regarding the anger that a few faculty members had expressed about my academic appointments and salary when I served as an assistant dean and later as an assistant provost, and the possibility of retaliation, if they were given the chance.

Fifth, Dr. Green asked me to withdraw my application because I will lack the support (presumably) from you and/or other higher-level decision makers, even if she chooses to "weakly support" my application. When I refused, she stated that my decision "was a mistake." I understood this to be a threat that I would never be promoted if I moved forward. You should know many departments use the "weakly support strategy" to cover their discriminatory deeds and pass the dirty work to upper administrators. I can only hope that you and others down the line see through this strategy if it is used. Nonetheless, I have no intention of withdrawing my application and will see this all the way to the end.

Above all, I have asked for nothing from the school other than to be treated fairly and consistently according to clear standards and past practices. So far, I have not been granted this request. As Dr. Hopkins was aware, I had a similar experience at the University of Louisville (UofL) where I had to ultimately file an Equal Employment Opportunity Commission (EEOC) complaint to require UofL to follow its standards and practices regarding my application for tenure/promotion. As the first and only African American, I maintained that the department was applying new and unreasonable standards to me that were not used in other cases, just as Dr. Green is. Ultimately, the dean and UofL sided with me, and I was granted tenure/promotion despite the recommendations of my department, department chair, and college committee. Ironically, at UofL, a new department chair had just taken the role and attempted to apply new and unreasonable standards though he had not served as chair during my five-years of performance, just like Dr. Green is doing.

My experiences have deepened my awareness of the strategies typically used against Black professors who are applying for tenure or promotion. Some departments find one thing that we have not achieved and then they make that the "chase your tail" goal, all the while promising future acceptance. For example, in our conversation, Dr. Green stated I can achieve her new standards after 2 more years. This is one of the major reasons there are very few of us in tenured or full professor roles. It is not lost on me that I am the only tenured or tenure-track African American faculty at the entire Bush School.

Fortunately, I met the challenges at the Bush School by working twice as hard, keeping up with publications, teaching, and research standards, while still serving administratively. A fellow professor and good friend once commented that I do "36 hours of work in the 24-hour workday". Because of the typical treatment experienced by far too many Black professors, I knew I had to. We know all too often that any weakness or gap would be the reason given for roadblocks that other professors readily and easily pass through. I had hoped that the Bush School would be different when my time for promotion came due, but so far it is nearly an exact repeat of UofL. As a result, I am taking the unusual step of asking you to look past the few faculty attempts to dismiss my great overall performance record, as Dr. Green intends to do. I ask that they use the same standards applied to all, especially those that the department applied to Dr. Vaughn and Dr. Gerber.

I am free to meet with you regarding these concerns at any time you are available. Thank you for your time.

APPENDIX B

Memo About Dr. Bright Faculty Application

From: Dr. Hopkins
To: Dean Ryan Crocker

What follows below is a review of the search process relevant to the appointment of Dr. Leonard Bright and my recommendation for extending an offer as an associate professor with tenure. Accompanying it are the following documents, the recommendation of the program director, the final report of the search committee, the report of the college promotion committee (CPC), Bright's vitae, his letter of interest in an appointment as associate professor with tenure, and external letters of recommendation. We also have a file copy of more extensive teaching, research and service materials related to his tenure and promotion consideration at his home institution, available at your request.

Search Process

Following extensive national advertising in general and specialized sources, including recruitment activities at the annual meeting of the American Political Science Association, the vacancy announcement for an assistant or tenured associate professor in Public Administration/Public Management yielded 52 applicants, all of whom were evaluated along position-related criteria in the announcement. The relevant search committee forwarded an analysis of three top candidates accompanied by supporting material and recommended that three interviews be conducted. The Committee reported that any of these finalists would be a welcome addition to the Bush School and that there were no obvious weaknesses in any of the finalist's files. This recommendation was supported by the department program director, the pool was certified by the Executive Associate Dean as robust and diverse, and the program director was authorized to proceed with interview invitations to candidates Leonard Bright, [other candidates names omitted].

Dr. [Name Omitted] withdrew her candidacy. The search committee issued a final report that unanimously concluded that both Bright and [name omitted] were acceptable for hiring, ordering [Name Omitted] first and Bright second, and further recommended that if an offer is extended to [Name Omitted] (as an assistant professor) and declined, an offer should be extended to Bright (as an advanced assistant professor). The report also summarized a survey of broader faculty sentiment (N=14) which indicated that, without objection, both candidates were acceptable for appointment. The full-time faculty of the College met to hear the search committee report and offer additional advice. In that meeting of 20 voting faculty both candidates were considered acceptable, with 16 favoring an offer to [name omitted] first and 4 favoring an offer to Bright first.

On December 20 I reported a positive recommendation to the dean to appoint [name omitted] as an assistant professor, coupled with appropriate credential materials and reports, a certification of the applicant pool and a certification that the search process was consistent with policy and guidelines, accompanied by the positive recommendation of the program director to extend an offer to [name omitted]. The dean approved this action, a verbal and draft written offer was extended shortly thereafter, and the offer was rejected.

Consistent with the chain of prior recommendations, offer conversations were initiated by the program director with Bright following my recommendation and that of the program director. The Director also relayed that Bright's record was superior to two recent promotions with tenure in the Bush School and that he should be treated as comparably as possible to a candidate with a similar record, but who had held the Ph.D. for a shorter period and was being offered a tenured associate professor position in international affairs. Following the dean's certification that Bright was *"impressive"* and that our DPC should convene immediately to consider the tenure question, I also requested that we seek information from Bright on his current promotion and tenure status at his home institution, the University of Louisville.

The program director discussed salary parameters with Bright as well as preferences for rank and tenure. Bright relayed favorable action on his promotion and tenure consideration at the University of Louisville, expressed his interest in a tenured associate professorship and offered to send his entire tenure packet (over 270 pages) to the program director. These additional extensive teaching, research and service materials were accompanied by a letter from Bright requesting support for tenure at Texas A&M and providing a comprehensive review of his career and accomplishments. At that time, the program director requested the chair of the college's promotion committee to review Bright's credentials with the committee to be considered for a tenured associate professorship. The record was bolstered by additional letters of recommendation from independent external scholars solicited by the Bush School. The resulting file on Bright included 17 letters of recommendation either provided by the University of Louisville, the candidate, or the Bush School, 13 of which were non-duplicative (2 in the Louisville file are duplicates of those submitted to TAMU by Bright and 2 duplicate those solicited by the department promotion committee).

Following receipt of these materials and new letters of recommendation, the CPC (11 of 12 tenured faculty) met to make an advisory recommendation. Unfortunately, the Committee was instructed incorrectly that there were two sets of choices, 1) to grant promotion without tenure (a resulting vote of 10 yes, 1 no), and 2) to grant or not grant tenure (a resulting vote of 3 in favor and 8 opposed).

The separation of tenure and the rank of associate professor is a highly uncommon occurrence in academe and by convention at Texas A&M. By institutional policy, a Texas A&M faculty member considered for promotion to associate professor cannot be granted the associate professor title without also holding tenure, i.e., the two are inseparable (SAP 12.01 .99.M2-4.3.3). Although University policy on external appointments is silent on this question, the Dean of Faculties confirmed that such a separation is *"very rare,"* that such is *"discouraged"* and that there is a *"strong preference"* to couple them. Indeed, in those unusual instances when exceptions might be made, it is almost always based on the lack of observable performance information on teaching for a candidate who has been in industry or other non-teaching academic settings for whom a probationary period is desirable in order to compensate for a clear deficiency. In addition, we were reminded that for someone as experienced as Bright, he would have a very brief remaining probationary period and that when candidates in this position are considered for tenure, it is often the case that expectations are unfairly heightened compared to others.

The Bush School has never had a faculty member, either through on-campus promotion or through an external hire, for whom tenure and promotion have been disconnected at this level, nor have prior promotion committees either been so instructed or acted in such a manner with other candidates attracted to the Bush School, to the best of my knowledge. Most important for Bright's consideration, there is no documented deficiency in his record that has been identified by anyone to warrant such an exception as he has been well-tested in teaching, research, and service over 8 years since receiving the Ph.D., including appointments at two different universities. In addition, the vacancy announcement for this position indicated clearly that, as conventional, the appointment would be made at either the assistant professor level or the tenured associate professor level. The reason offered by the Promotion Committee for this otherwise unknowingly rare recommendation of promotion to associate without tenure was based on the narrow view that Bright had *"the potential to publish in the two leading journals in the field."* As shown below, there is a view that his work is of sufficiently high quality to appear in such sources, but that he instead published in the top sub-field journals and with considerable impact. Furthermore, there is no such narrowly prescribed publication requirement for tenure in either policy or practice at the Bush School.

The only option for the Promotion Committee to have considered was one of either tenure or no tenure on arrival as further reflected in college search guidelines. It is important to note the above process irregularity in light of this latest advisory vote.

Teaching Experience and Performance

Leonard Bright has been teaching full-time at the university level, in addition to having had part-time prior experience in the classroom. He has taught a full range of courses central to our public administration curriculum, especially public personnel management, policy analysis, the fundamentals of public administration, program evaluation, organization behavior, leadership, workplace diversity and nonprofit management. As shown in his record, his courses are rigorous, diverse in pedagogical approaches and well received. Syllabi in the record are well crafted and peer reviews of his classroom performance are positive (based on visitations). Student evaluations of his teaching are generally in the 4.0 range (on a 5 point scale), with many often higher. The full record of his student evaluations of teaching over the years is available in his file. Bright is clearly conscientious and thoughtful about his teaching as further reflected in his experimentation with various approaches and participation in workshops on teaching. This thoughtfulness and commitment to teaching is further exemplified by his analysis of his own instructional experiences contained in his letter which is accompanied by additional extensive documentation relevant to his favorable tenure decision at his home institution.

Research Experience and Performance

Leonard Bright has established a quantitatively and qualitatively meritorious and impactful research record as a junior scholar. He has had ten refereed publications, to include eight journal articles that have either appeared or have been scheduled for publication and two book chapters. In addition to a book review, Bright has presented a dozen papers at professional meetings, most of which are refereed, and received several competitive internal grant awards to support his research. This rate of peer-reviewed research activity exceeds or is comparable to that of junior faculty who have been tenured at the Bush School and comparable to the records of external candidates to whom a tenured associate professorship offer has been made. In addition, based upon conventional measures of research impact-the extent to which work is cited by other scholars-Bright's research has been well received and influential in the field, as noted by over 100 citations to his refereed research. As noted by external reviewers, this is an unusually high rate, and it is one that typically exceeds citations of junior faculty research at the Bush School.

We are fortunate to have considerable independent scholarly views of Bright's research through the availability of an unprecedented 17 letters or recommendation solicited through a variety of means, nine primarily by the University of Louisville as part of his tenure review process, four submitted as part of his original application to the Bush School, and an additional four that were specially solicited by the School's Promotion

Committee. Although four of these appear to be from duplicate authors, this is an extraordinarily large set of external reviews. Not one of these reviewers is negative about Bright's research or recommends against tenure as an associate professor. This is a remarkable achievement from 13 different individuals who are independent scholars, most of whom were selected by parties other than the candidate. A few referees do not specifically comment on the tenure decision since they did not have access to other performance factors beyond research. Several themes clearly emerge with some consistency across these numerous reviews.

- Bright publishes consistently in the top specialty journals in his sub-field (public personnel management).

- The pace of his publication is steady.

- The quantity of his publications is acceptable to high.

- His research is of high quality and some pieces could have warranted placement in one of the top two more general academic journals in public administration.

- He has established himself as the leading national scholar on public service motivation.

- He has researched independently as a scholar, with most of his publications being single-authored and therefore a clear indication of his personal and independent capabilities.

- His research work is focused and builds a cumulative body of knowledge.

- His research work is empirical and often based on original data collection.

- His research record would likely have been even more extensive if he had been in a different type of public affairs school rather than in a college of business or if he had not been in settings with such a heavy teaching and administrative load.

Service Experience

Leonard Bright has an extensive campus and professional service record, which is unusual for such an early stage in his career, and in all dimensions, it rivals or exceeds service expectations of newly tenured faculty at the Bush School. On campus, he has been an assistant director of a graduate public administration program and has been active on admissions, diversity, comprehensive exam, budget, library, program development and grievance committees at the departmental level. This is complemented by college-level service on an academic standards committee and university service in admissions, faculty recruitment and as an active member of the African American Mentor Program. His service to both the profession and community is evidenced by his role as president of the Louisville chapter of his national professional association (American Society for Public Administration), bringing together academics, practitioners, and students in significant professional activities. Even more impactful, as a junior faculty member, he spent two years in a leadership role planning and executing the anniversary meeting of the Southeastern Conference for Public Administration. All of this is in addition to his considerable professional conference roles as a presenter and as a manuscript reviewer for academic journals.

In summary, the decision to grant tenure for a faculty member is based on both the candidate's comprehensive and cumulative record in all dimensions-teaching, research, and service-and on a forecast of continued success as an academic. Leonard Bright has clearly met the test on all three dimensions. The issue of placement of his publications, which are of documented high quality and impact, in more general top tier public administration sources should be viewed as an especially narrow consideration. Furthermore, it is one neither consistently practiced in the Bush School nor especially meaningful since Bright has published in the top tier specialty journals in his field, along with publications in second tier journals. It should also be noted that he has taught and researched most recently in a comprehensive urban university that offers a full range of degrees in public affairs-bachelors, master's, and doctorate-and he has experience at all levels. Although successful at the University of Louisville, his administrative location is within a school focused heavily on urban affairs (rather than public administration) within a college of business. I forecast that Leonard Bright will flourish even more in an environment like that provided by the Bush School and Texas A&M.

APPENDIX C
Dr. Bright Full Promotion Application Letter

Introduction

I am applying for promotion to full professor in Texas A&M's the Bush School of Government. I have 15 years of experience as a tenured and tenure-track professor. The Bush School is a master's only terminal degree program with a mission to develop principled leaders for public service. My career goals and accomplishments fit this mission perfectly. I started my academic career with a game plan to excel in research, teaching, and service, and to gain formal applied leadership experience along the way. Ultimately, I believe that I have made notable impacts in these areas as exemplified by my national and international research reputation, quality, and range of courses I have taught, multiple sustained leadership contributions I have made to my profession and department, and years of progressive administrative experience as an Assistant Director, assistant dean, and assistant provost.

Research

I am a specialist when it comes to research. I have focused on questions relating to work motivation among government employees, the effects of public service motivation on management outcomes, and the efficacy of public administration education on student career interests. I have produced 14 peer-reviewed journal publications, and one book chapter, and I also have several manuscripts in the peer-review process and in the early stages of development. I have maintained first author status in all of my publications, with 80% being single authored. My outlets are among the top ten U.S. based journals in public management, and industrial and labor relations (e.g., ARPA,

PPM, & ROPPA), and in leading peer-reviewed public administration education journals (JPAE & TPA). Below are examples of my research impact and future plans.

<u>Public Service Motivation (PSM)</u>: My primary research impact centers in PSM. My scholarship has helped clarify the scope and impact of PSM in government organizations. In the early years, many believed that PSM offered only positive direct benefits in public organizations, despite the fact that there were published studies to the contrary. Most of these studies were also limited by their reliance on proxy measures of PSM (i.e., sector of work, and job satisfaction). I was among the first scholars to demonstrate that PSM had measurable impacts on important organizational outcomes using Perry's PSM measurement scale. I collected firsthand data from local and state governments in Oregon, Indiana, and Kentucky, and produced six publications that compared the effects of PSM on a range of organizational outcomes and behaviors. My findings demonstrated that 1) PSM was not the only important predictor of employee behaviors when compared to other predictors, such as management level and person organizational fit; 2) PSM was a strong reason why public employees desired intrinsic non-monetary work opportunities; 3) individuals with high levels of PSM were not congruent in all types of public settings; and 4) incongruence leads to negative consequences for employee behaviors, notwithstanding the influence of PSM.

<u>Public Administration Education</u>: My second line of research focused on understanding how the socialization experiences of students in graduate programs influence a range of attitudes and behaviors. I produced six publications that are based on data gathered from a national survey I conducted on 26 public affairs graduate programs. The findings of this research suggest that 1) interest in government careers among graduate students are declining from entry to graduation from MPA programs, 2)

graduate students with high levels of PSM are significantly more interested in nonprofit careers than government careers, 3) degree program characteristics were meaningfully related to students level of PSM, 4) In-service students are significantly less satisfied in public administration programs than pre-service students, and 5) the methodological requirements of degree programs were related to students perceptions of their fit in government organizations and their interest in government careers.

Additional Research: I have produced a journal publication and a book chapter that centered on general work motivation. The journal publication entitled *"Why Age Matters?"* explored the relationship between chronological age and work preferences from the standpoints of generational differences, level of access, and socialization. I wanted to understand the extent to which generational differences/personalities were the most important explanation for the effects of age when compared to other explanations. The results suggested that generational differences were the least important explanation of age-differences when compared to level of access and socialization, which was operationalized as management level and years of work experience, respectively. These findings helped place the effects of generational differences within a proper context. In addition, I produced a book chapter that explored various theories of intrinsic motivation and its effects on organizational behavior in public organizations. I have used this framework to guide my research on the topic.

Other Research Indicators: I have made important contributions to the scholarship in my field of research, as demonstrated by the rate and pattern of the citations to my publications. I have a robust Google Scholar and Web of Science citation rate (i.e., 1200+ and 600+, respectively). Citations to my research is attributed to scholars from a wide range of countries (e.g., U.S., South Korea, China, Denmark, & Switzerland) and originate from top-tier journals in my field (e.g., PAR & JPART). For example, according to the Web of Science, research published in PAR is the single highest source of citations of my research. Additionally, I have received invitations to assist local, national, and international agencies on matters pertaining to my expertise in PSM and work motivation. For example, research foundation invited me to review a project on PSM proposed by researchers. The Federal Transportation Security Administration (TSA) invited me to help them improve the motivational conditions of their front-line employees in Oregon. This partnership has resulted in the development of a major data collection study, and opportunities to advise Oregon's Federal Executive Board and TSA executives.

Above all, I am pleased that my colleagues in the Bush School noted that my research performance *"clearly exceeded the level associated with a satisfactory rating"* during my post-tenure review. I have plans to build on this success in the future. For example, the data I collected from the TSA is the basis of three manuscripts that are in the peer review process and several others which are at various stages of development. Subsequently, I have engaged in a second project with the TSA that involves a longitudinal study that explores the effects of various treatments designed to deepen organizational commitment and PSM levels. I will have several manuscripts from this project in the peer review process. Similarly, I followed up my second line of research on the socialization experiences of MPA students with a second round of national surveys. I plan to use this new data, along with the data collected in 2014, to complete a book that explores strategies for improving the fit between students and government careers using an educational socialization framework.

Teaching

I am a generalist when it comes to teaching public administration. I have taught a wide range of courses, such as leadership theory and practice, nonprofit management, organizational theory and behavior, program evaluation, public management, public policy, and workplace diversity. My courses are very interactive, and discussion based. I expect my students to learn, think critically, communicate their thoughts clearly and concisely, and appreciate the value of evidence-based decision-making. I am also interested in deepening the value that students have of public service careers, especially given existing research that suggests that public administration programs are struggling to accomplish this goal. I have found that students learn these skills and habits of the heart best when given the opportunity to experiment with real-world issues. My interest in using experimental learning led to a publication entitled Nonprofit Outreach Services in Year 3. I have used many of the techniques outlined in this article in my classes. Below are examples of my teaching impact.

Nonprofit Management: This course explores the stages of developing a nonprofit organization from the *"ground up."* Students are required to develop a nonprofit business plan by focusing on its mission, vision, funding, and structure. One of my students used this course to start a new nonprofit organization in Louisville Kentucky that addresses the capacity of communities, schools, and families to prepare young adults for the workforce. I served as one of the first members of the board of directors. Today, the agency remains active.

Program Evaluation: I designed this course to explore the topic of program evaluation from three major perspectives (i.e., problem structuring, logic modeling, and evaluation strategies), using an agency of interest. Basically, students must develop a concise problem path model that delineates the causal relationships that make up the situation their agency was created to address; a clear logic model that links inputs, activities, outputs, and impacts of their agency's strategies; and an evaluation plan that can empirically measure the impact that their agency is having on the problems it was created to address. At the end of the course, students must demonstrate proficiency in completing literature reviews, articulating their own assumptions and major theories that underlie their interpretations, and understanding of the strengths and weaknesses of various methodological approaches. This is the only course that I am aware of that integrates problem structuring as a major component of program evaluation. In addition, students often use this course as a model for their capstone projects in the Bush School. I experimented with the use of peer assessments of graded assignments, based on research that demonstrated its positive effects on student learning. While I noticed that subject matter comprehension increased, my student evaluations were lower than average during these two terms.

Workplace Diversity: I overhauled this course to emphasize theories of inclusion, organizational barriers to diversity management, and the phenomenological experiences of minority characteristics (e.g., gender, race, sexual orientation, disability, religion, and communication styles). I worked to create a class environment of openness that allowed a range of points of views to be heard, understood, and possibly appreciated. My assignments sought to increase students' awareness of their own uniqueness, understanding of the experiences of others, and ability to address inequality within an organizational context. For example, one assignment required students to describe their own ethnic histories and share them with the class. Another assignment required students to diagnose the ethnic and gender integration that exists within a local public or non-profit organization and develop mitigating solutions. NASPAA COPRA site reviewers described this course as *"an outstanding elective on diversity."*

Capstones Seminars. I advised two-year-long capstone courses. Our capstones require students to apply the comprehensive set of knowledge and skills they have acquired in our degree program to a client-sponsored issue. This includes working with the client to define a problem, executing a research strategy for addressing that issue, and presenting a professional report that serves the client's needs. I approach my capstones from an organizational framework. I supply my team with the end of program goals/targets, assign working roles, and expect them to work through the formative requirements of the project with only advice from me. My first capstone class explored the drivers of Cambodia's history and socioeconomic conditions, and strategies for measuring the outputs and impact of our client's strategies in Cambodia. Four of the students travelled to Cambodia to conduct firsthand interviews and surveys. I was pleased that my team received the American Society for Public Administration (ASPA) CenTex James W. McGrew Research Award out of over 20 other capstones that year.

<u>Center for the Integration of Research, Teaching, and Learning (CIRTL)</u>. In addition to my formal teaching responsibilities in the Bush School, I have served in Texas A&M's CIRTL program as the institutional co-leader and an instructor. CIRTL is a multi-institutional consortium that seeks to improve the teaching skills of our doctoral students and postdocs. I am the lead instructor and mentor in CIRTL MOOC entitled *"An Introduction to Evidence-Based Teaching."* This course covers a broad range of principles and techniques that include assessing student learning, inclusive teaching approaches, and lesson planning.

In sum, my students and colleagues have favorably noted the impact of my teaching. My student evaluations at the Bush School have averaged 4.5 out of 5 points. Additionally, I was very happy to receive the ASPA CenTex Chapter's Distinguished Public Administration Educator Award from my colleagues.

Service

I have always placed a high value on being a good citizen to my profession, faculty, and administration.

Profession: I am a regular reviewer for many journals in my field, serve as an editorial board member for ROPPA and PPM, and have chaired various ASPA and Southeastern Conference on Public Administration (SECOPA) related committees. I have also had the opportunity to serve as the president of two major professional organizations, Metropolitan Louisville ASPA and SECOPA. In these roles, I worked with faculty and officials across the southeastern U.S. region to develop academic conferences, fundraising and endowment activities, and fellowships.

Faculty: As a faculty member, I have participated on a myriad of councils, committees, and task forces that address a variety of issues, such as faculty and student grievances, fundraising and development, strategic planning and budgeting, and information technology. One of my most rewarding experiences was my service as a faculty senator at Texas A&M, with two years on the executive committee of the senate.

Administration: I have seven years of formal administrative experience at three major public universities as an Assistant Director of the MPA program at the University of South Alabama, assistant dean in the Bush School, and assistant provost in the Office of Graduate Studies at Texas A&M. These experiences not only gave me the opportunity to positively influence graduate education at the department, college, and university levels, it has also enhanced my research and teaching of leadership and motivation topics.

Furthermore, my service activities have been favorably recognized over the years. I was pleased to receive the ASPA Chester A. Newland Presidential Citation of Merit in 2013, and the

Appendix C

Stadelmann Faculty Senate Service Award from my peers in recognition of my service to my profession and faculty, respectively.

APPENDIX D

The External Reviewer Letters Collected

Reviewer 1

I am providing an external review of Associate Professor Leonard Bright for promotion to the rank of professor.

First, I should mention that I have only met Professor Bright a few times that I can recall. We are both frequent participants at the same professional conferences (e.g., ASPA, SECOPA), where Dr. Bright often has a prominent role. Professor Bright's body of work to date coincides closely with scholarly and administrative interests of mine focusing on ethics, public service values and public management strategies.

Dr. Bright's best known for his work on public service motivation (PSM) which is a prominent focus of the articles in his promotion packet. In several of these articles he uses PSM as an independent variable to help explain student satisfaction with their degree program, interest in government and nonprofit careers, and government work environments, while controlling for other explanatory variables. I was especially impressed by his sole-authored and co-authored articles dealing with graduate student satisfaction with public administration degree programs and those exploring student decisions related to career interest/choice. My interest in these pieces is no doubt related to my 40 years of experience as graduate director of a public administration program and concern about how best to attract and serve our students.

The quality of Dr. Bright's scholarship is evident in the care he takes to clarify concepts and clearly explain his theoretical arguments, always well-grounded in relevant literature. In these articles, he employs appropriate analytical and statistical methods, highlights key findings, and demonstrates their contributions to theory and public administration education practice. He has a knack for identifying gaps in the literature and designing studies which contribute new knowledge and insights that inform both scholarship and professional practice. While the journal placement of his articles (Public Personnel insights that inform both scholarship and professional practice. While the journal placement of his articles (Public Personnel Management, Journal of Public Affairs Education, Teaching Public Administration) is appropriate to the subjects addressed and to his intended target audience (professional practitioners and public service educators), their visibility is somewhat limited given that his most recent work is not found in the general public administration journals with wider readership. His three earlier publications in general journals like the American Review of Public Administration and top-quality specialty journals like Review of Public Personnel Administration account for 77 percent of his Google Scholar citations. Nonetheless, his 1221 Google Scholar cites (878 since 2013) show that his published work is having a significant impact equal to or higher than that of others seeking promotion to full professor at comparable institutions. In this sense, his recent articles are under-placed, and their contribution deserves a wider readership but taking into account the quantity and quality of his overall scholarly production, his record clearly warrants promotion to professor.

Focusing more specifically on his sole-authored and co-authored articles dealing with graduate student satisfaction in public administration programs, the articles very effectively establish the significance of the problem, summarize relevant literature, identify predictors of student attitudes, explain the research methods, report findings, consider implications and draw reasonable conclusions. Important findings explaining student satisfaction are identified as support from their degree program, program climate and years of experience in government. This is confirmed by my experience as a program director and consistent with expectations from the literature.

While all the explanatory variables were clearly identified and carefully justified, I would have been interesting to see if there were differences between programs located in private vs. public universities where cost differences may partially explain student satisfaction. Our student exit surveys suggest this is an important factor here. I intend to survey our graduate PA students using the program climate survey questions to compare results with those reported for the 26 schools in this study. This is one indication of what I see as the relevance and practical benefit from such research beyond its contribution to scholarship.

An impressive feature of Dr. Bright's package is how the articles build on one another with findings from one piece leading to questions that are addressed in subsequent articles. It is very helpful to see how the influence of PSM and other variables explain career preferences in government in one article and then see how the same variables explain such preferences in nonprofit organizations. An important, and surprising finding here is that individuals with high PSM prefer nonprofit careers over government careers, which Bright suggests may be partially explained by the way PSM is conceptualized and measured, recently in more expansive ways at his prompting. Dr. Bright's research also contributes to scholarship on person-work environment (PE fit) with the first empirical text exploring the link between PSM and person-organization fit (PO fit) as well as person-job fit (PJ fit). He finds that increases in respondents' PSM is associated with more compatible PO and PJ fit, and that PSM was a better predictor of PO fit than PJ fit. In this and other studies he expands on existing literature offering promising new directions for research to guide subsequent scholarly studies on PSM and its association with other attitudes, perceptions, and behavior.

In short, Dr. Bright has a coherent, well-integrated research agenda and a trajectory of steady scholarly productivity over time, establishing his national reputation as a leading expert on public service motivation and public administration education.

A review of his CV and personal statement indicates his versatility as a teacher and his extraordinary service-related contributions, the latter far exceeding that of most academics at a comparable career stage. His service-related efforts have been recognized with awards and prestigious positions from ASPA at the national level (the Chester A. Newland Presidential Citation of Merit), SECOPA (service as President) at the regional level, and ASPA chapter (Distinguished PA Educator Award) at the local level. He has also served as the assistant provost and assistant dean at the Bush School along with a number of important roles he has played at his current and former universities and in professional organizations.

In terms of the pattern of productivity and quantity of peer publications, Professor Bright has seven refereed journal articles (four sole-authored) post-tenure and another seven articles (six sole authored) pre-tenure. He has also published a book chapter and book review, received several internal and external grants, and made more than two dozen paper presentations at professional conferences. This level of productivity clearly meets the Promotion guidelines for research. His scholarly productivity and the teaching and service record he has developed meets the standard for faculty at similar stages of their careers at the university where I currently work or where I have previously worked. In summary, this is a solid record in terms of the number and quality of publications together with his extensive teaching, service, and administrative contributions. I recommend that he be promoted to professor.

I hope these comments are useful for Professor Bright's promotion review.

Reviewer 2

This letter provides an evaluation of the scholarship of Professor Leonard Bright as part of consideration for his promotion to full professor.

Let me note that while I was once a faculty member at the Bush School, I have not collaborated with Professor Bright, nor have I had any professional or personal interactions with him. I know him only through his professional work, some of which I had previously read, and some of which I read as part of his review package. This is, therefore, a fully arms-length letter.

Professor Bright is best known for his contributions to the study of public service motivation (PSM). In particular, a handful of papers map out the relationship between work conditions, motivations, and employee outcomes. His most cited work, Does Public Service Motivation Really Make a Difference on the Job Satisfaction and Turnover Intentions of Public Employees show that PSM's effects on key measures of employee satisfaction is contingent on person-organization fit. Another way of understanding this result is that selection effects (people who want to work in public organizations select into those organizations) explain the positive effects of PSM on public employee outcomes. He explores similar territory in Does Person-Organization Fit Mediate the Relationship Between Public Service Motivation and the Job Performance of Public Employees? The paper Public Employees with High Levels of Public Service Motivation, Who Are They, Where Are They, and What Do They Want? provides a deeper understanding of the characteristics of employees with high PSM.

Together, these three papers represent the majority of Professor Bright's citations. Why are they so important? Partly it is because they were timely, arriving at a moment when the empirical study of PSM was taking off. While the papers had data limitations, they were also theoretically nuanced, considering the mediating relationships of an employee's relationship with their organization on the effects of PSM. Bright drew concepts from mainstream organizational studies, and fit them into the nascent study of PSM, thereby elevating the quality of the analysis. Future work on the topic has acknowledged the mediating role of person-organization fit, and other factors. A profound practical lesson of this work, which I have cited, is that recruiting employees with high PSM will only pay off if public organizations also ensure that they find ways to cultivate that desire to serve. Organizational conditions that create a distance between the employee's expectations and what they are asked to do in practice wastes the potential benefits of PSM.

For these reasons, Professor Bright deserves to be considered as an important scholar in the study of public service motivation, and of public personnel more broadly. His work is internationally known.

His most recent publications reflect both his general interest in motivation in public affairs, but perhaps also his growing administrative role. Since 2009, most of his publications have been in Teaching Public Administration, Journal of Public Affairs Education, and Public Personnel Management. These are less high-profile venues, and less likely to have the scholarly impact that his work from Year 1. They are, however, a way of reaching a broader professional audience that reflects his current administrative positions.

These more recent publications tell us more about the aspirations of students in professional MPA programs. His most recent work still captures previous themes. For example, he shows that the interests of students in MPA programs are driven by a perception that government is where they can pursue their values. In part, this is why many with especially high public service motivation are seeking the non-profit route (Is Public Service Motivation a Better Explanation of Nonprofit Career

Preferences Than Government Career Preferences?) An important implication is that if public-service individuals stop seeing those values represented they become less likely to select into government (Government Career Interests). They also offer interesting insights for public affairs educators, such as the fact that those who are less interested in programs with methods courses are more interested in public sector work. In another study, he shows that more experienced MPA students are more likely to be dissatisfied. Such insights are quite useful for the NAPSAA community working in public affairs schools.

I also found his new paper on military veterans highly interesting (Does Military Experience Influence the Work Attitudes and Behaviors of Federal Employees?) It's a well-established claim that the high number of veterans in government tend to be less satisfied with non-military public work than fellow employees, but with little evidence as to why. Using a sample of state level homeland security employees, Bright makes a persuasive case that once we control for other demographic and career factors associated with being a veteran, military experience is not, in itself, a significant predictor of dissatisfaction. Such analysis helps to provide a better understanding of how to deal with sources of veteran dissatisfaction, and it would be desirable to see it replicated in other settings, which I hope he considers pursuing.

Across his body of work, there is a remarkable consistency in themes and approaches. He takes an applied empirical approach. Rather than develop new theory, he seeks to synthesize existing frameworks from public administration and organization theory, which requires some skill and knowledge of these different fields. He almost always works on survey-based cross-sectional designs, usually with data that he himself has collected. The analysis is appropriate given the nature of the data. There is the issue of common method bias, though many of his primary variables are demographic, and so less susceptible to social desirability bias that fuels artificially high correlations that drive common method bias. His papers are clear in their intent and well written.

The most striking characteristic of his work is that he takes on some observed or expected public sector personal relationship - often between motivation or a demographic characteristic on the one hand, and sector selection or satisfaction on the other -and seeks to offer deeper insight into the nature of that relationship. In some cases, he points to previously unappreciated mediators (such as person-organization fit) and in other cases he offers evidence that expected relationships don't actually exist once we control for other observable factors.

Given my limited interactions with Professor Bright, I cannot offer any assessment of his teaching. He has clearly been actively engaged in service at his own institution as assistant dean of the Bush School and now assistant provost at Texas A&M University. He has also provided service to the field as the President of the Southeastern Conference on Public Administration. This pattern of service runs consistently throughout his career.

Overall, I think his work is careful, well-done, and useful for the field of public affairs. I am favorably disposed toward his promotion. His work has been cited 1,225 times according to Google Scholar. This is a good number for most professors at this stage of his career. It is also notable that Professor Bright tends to engage in sole-authored work, which is increasingly unusual, and requires extra time and effort to produce a single paper, especially when relying on self-collected data. Perhaps working more frequently with co-authors or PhD students would allow him to generate more publications even as he maintains his significant service responsibilities.

Please do not hesitate in contacting me if you have any questions.

Reviewer 3

This responds to your request for an evaluation of Dr. Leonard Bright's record in relation to his candidacy for promotion to full professor. I have carefully reviewed the records and the materials you sent me. I have written many of these letters for candidates at large research universities, such as Minnesota, North Carolina, Ohio State, Pennsylvania State, Rutgers, Vanderbilt, and others. I served on my institution's university-level promotion and tenure review committee for the social and behavioral sciences for three recent years. There I observed the successful records of candidates from different social scientific and administrative fields and the criteria applied by external reviewers and faculty in those fields. I have observed that the typical successful candidate for promotion to full professor at a high-quality research university has published a minimum of 20 to 25 academic journal articles in high-quality journals. Often the successful candidate has published at least one book that met high academic standards, although the requirement for a book has seemed less important at major universities in recent years. Review committees typically ask for assurances of the quality and impact of the candidate's contributions.

Dr. Bright has published 14 articles, a book chapter, and a book review since Year 1, the approximate number of years since completion of his doctorate. He has also produced reports and other publications. This level of research productivity in the number of publications, compared to other candidates for full professor at leading programs and universities, is well below average.

The more important criteria involve the quality and apparent impact of the candidate's publications and scholarly contributions. Two of the candidate's articles have appeared in Review of Public Personnel Administration, three in Public Personnel Management, and one in American Review of Public Administration. In public administration, these journals are considered respectable journals of sound quality, and as second tier journals. Dr. Bright has published three recent articles in Teaching Public Administration. This journal is published by Sage publications, a well-established publisher. A journal ranking service that I looked up on-line ranks this journal 90th out of 130 journals in public administration. Several additional articles have appeared in the Journal of Public Affairs Education. I am not closely familiar with this journal, but I have been aware of it as an on-line publication. It has recently come into publication under the auspices of NASPAA, the leading international association for administrative and policy issues (such as program accreditation) in public administration and public affairs. I am not certain of its ranking or citation rate. The record shows no publication in a top-tier journal. Review committees typically take such aspects of the record into account, especially at top tier universities such as Texas A&M.

According to Google Citations, Dr. Bright's articles have been cited about 1243 times as of the writing of this review. In public administration and public affairs, where citation rates tend to be lower than in other fields, this is a respectable citation rate, that approximates the citation rate of rising associate professors working toward qualification for promotion to professor.

The evidence described above indicates that the quality of this record is below average in comparison to successful candidates for promotion to full professor in programs in public administration and public affairs at research universities in the United States. It is not comparable to the standards that I have observed for a leading university and program such as Texas A&M and the Bush School.

Dr. Bright is active at professional conferences. His record shows that he is active in grant-seeking and grant-getting. The record shows energetic participation in university service and administration. Dr. Bright has served in administrative roles which appear to involve significant responsibilities.

I met Dr. Bright once, at a professional conference. I felt that he represented your university very well. I do not know him well personally.

Your letter asking for this evaluation posed a number of specific questions. The paragraphs above respond to those questions. I will respond more directly to each question upon request.

Texas A&M University serves as one of the very high-quality academic institutions in the U.S. and the world. The Bush School serves as one of the most valuable institutions in the field to which I am devoted. Faculty members at the Bush School include professional colleagues in whom I hold the highest esteem. I submit this evaluation with these considerations in mind.

Reviewer 4

Thank you very much for requesting my evaluation of the research and publications of Dr. Leonard Bright as you consider his promotion from the rank of associate professor to the rank of professor in the department in the Bush School of Government and Public Service at Texas A&M University. I write a number of letters like this every year, and I am well acquainted with the norms of research productivity and scholarly visibility associated with promotion to ranks above the entry level at research-oriented universities. I do not know Dr. Bright personally. I do not recall if I have ever met him, but I have seen some of his work on public service motivation that appeared in the Review of Public Personnel Administration and the American Review of Public Administration.

In preparing for this report, I carefully reviewed Dr. Bright's vitae and the cover letter he submitted, and I have read all the articles that were included in the package you sent to me. I find some of Professor Bright's research thoughtful and intriguing, and I will comment on those pieces shortly. However, I note that Dr. Bright has published only 14 referred journal articles and one book chapter. In addition, most of the articles are placed in lower-level outlets. For example, there are 3 articles in Teaching Public Administration, a journal published in the UK that is not widely read in the United States and is by any consideration a third- or fourth-tier periodical. There are also 3 articles published in the Journal of Public Affairs Education, an outlet currently produced by NASPAA, but not one that is a major source of research in the field. Five articles are published in Public Personnel Management, a better outlet, but still one that is at best second tier. Journals with the most visibility on Dr. Bright's vitae are the American Review of Public Administration (n= 1) and the Review of Public Personnel Administration (n=2). These are both good outlets, but they account for only 3 publications. The record is devoid of publications in leading journals such as the Journal of Public Administration Research and Theory or Public Administration Review. Thus, the research record is weak. The number of publications is small for a scholar being considered for promotion to the rank of professor, and no work appears in the top journals in the field. In addition, there is no book, although I would not consider that mandatory, and there is only 1 piece published as a book chapter. I realize that almost all the work is sole authored, but still, this is a record that is thin and has not developed sufficiently, in my opinion, to have a substantial impact on the field. I cannot at this point consider Dr. Bright a leading figure in the discipline. That level of status and recognition could develop, but it will require continued work and a more active research posture.

I believe Dr. Bright is a capable scholar. That fact is demonstrated by some of his early work. For example, his work on public service motivation (PSM) and the job performance of public employees, published in the Review of Public Personnel Administration, is well conceived and well-executed empirical research on an important issue. Bright's finding, that when an employee's congruence or fit with their organization is considered, the positive relationship between PSM and job performance disappears, is important This piece made a meaningful contribution to the literature on public service motivation and is an example of the kind of research needed in the field. Other work on PSM and job satisfaction, such as the piece published in the American Review of Public Administration, also represents a solid contribution. More work of this nature on other important issues in the field would help considerably in building Dr. Bright's record.

I understand that Dr. Bright has held administrative positions, and I know from personal experience that responsibilities of that nature can drive out time needed for research and publication. Nevertheless, as the record now stands, I believe it falls short of what is normally expected for the rank of professor.

Reviewer 5

Thank you for the opportunity to review the promotion file for associate professor Leonard Bright. He is applying for the rank of full professor in the Bush School of Government and Public Service at Texas A&M University. I do not know Dr. Bright personally, professionally, or reputationally. I also was unaware of most of his work prior to receiving the complete file you sent to me. I have now had time to read his body of work, place it in the context of the criteria you mention in your cover letter, and evaluate his body of work in light of promotion requirements for full professor in other top 10 to 20 public administration and policy programs in the United States. I feel qualified to make these comparisons.

I regret to write that, while solid for an associate professorship and showing promise for future promotion to full professor, I cannot conclude that Dr. Bright yet meets the standards for promotion to full professor. Dr. Bright's record falls short in terms of quantity of publications relative to those at peer institutions but, most importantly, in terms of journal placement and/or university press publications and the reputational rewards that publication in those outlets brings. Basically, I agreed with the 2017 post-tenure review done by his colleagues at the Bush School that Dr. Bright *"clearly exceeded the level associated with a satisfactory rating"* (Promotion Cover Letter, p. 2). But, based on my judgement and experiences at two of the leading public affairs programs in the country (American University and the University of Georgia), there is insufficient evidence presented in his file that his record presently meets the research publication standards for promotion to full professor.

First, however, let me address the strengths of Dr. Bright's research record. These are strengths that give promise of promotion in the future if followed by additional productivity, better journal/book placement, continuing theory-driven rigor in those publications, and greater visibility in leadership positions in national professional associations. For starters, his work on public service motivation (PSM) has been published in respected mid-tier general public administration journals such as the American Review of Public Administration (ARPA). At the time, his work on PSM shows command of a variety of research literatures and theory, including business management, psychology, and education. I find this an especially important trait indicating intellectual curiosity, the absence of stovepiping of research thinking, and the ability to integrate both theory and attention to practice in his research. I also find that Dr. Bright has done some needed and insightful unpacking of the early conventional wisdom about PSM. He does so by statistically controlling for variables excluded in prior PSM research. His work suggests the need for conceptual and theoretical rethinking by scholars studying PSM in public and nonprofit organizations, as well as PSM's effects and incorporation in public affairs education. For example, his suggestion that organization-personality fit is a mediating factor to the effects of PSM is intriguing, important, and should garner additional attention and development.

Dr. Bright's most-cited PSM-related research is in ARPA, the Review of Public Personnel Administration (ROPPA), and Public Personnel Management. Because these articles are the most recent research he has done, the significant numbers of citations he already has will continue to grow over time. This will allow him to carve out a niche for himself in this currently vibrant research agenda. Ritz, Brewer, and Neumann (*"Public service motivation, A systematic literature review and outlook,"* Public Administration Review, 76,3, 414-426) find, for example, that over 50 journal articles have appeared on this topic annually since the early 1990s. This is important, because one is likely to get more citations when publishing on topical areas where research is being done. Based on this, I also would anticipate that his most-cited articles on PSM are likely to continue growing in citation counts. One caveat on these counts, it is important to be aware that considerable overlap exists between Google Scholar (GS) and Web of Science (WOS) citation counts. Specifically, Meho & Yang found that the overlap between WOS and Scopus was 58.2%. The overlap between GS and the union of WOS and Scopus was only 30.8%. Thus, the totals for the two citation services that Dr. Bright lists in his Promotion Cover Letter should not simply be added together. Moreover, because WOS is less inclusive of journals, GS typically shows higher citation rates. Still, citation counts for his top articles are suggestive of impact and, in my judgment, should spark additional research done by him and others.

That said, Dr. Bight seems to have already established a niche (joining with a growing number of researchers) for contrarian refinements of the theory and application of PSM that he can build on in future research. For example, his research shows that (contrary to original claims by Perry and Wise, 1990), PSM may apply more to nonprofit organizations. I also applaud the way Dr. Bright has tried to test and assess the impact of PSM on public affairs curricula, including its implications for student experiences. His articles in the Journal of Public Affairs Education (JPAE) and Teaching Public Administration, for instance, control for factors that affect such things as social support systems and again suggest that PSM claims must be qualified. They also suggest the importance of new or expanded use of interaction of students with the world of practice. Nonetheless, and importantly, Dr. Bright cautions against generalizing from his findings given the conceptual and methodological shortcomings in them (see more below).

Despite these positives, I regret to write that significant gaps exist in Dr. Bright's record that makes promotion to full professor problematic for me and, most likely, for others at peer-competitor institutions where I have served on the faculty. First, as noted earlier, he has thus far failed to publish in the top journals of his field, most notably in the Public Administration Review (PAR) and/or the Journal of Public Administration Research and Theory (JPART). He notes in his Promotion Cover Letter that his research has been cited in these journals, which is positive. But that clearly is not the same as Dr. Bright publishing in them. Moreover, for promotion to full professor at top-tier institutions where I have served on the faculty, publications in PAR and JPART and other mid-tier but respected journals are expected to be multiple and consistent over the years. Certainly, ROPPA is probably the leading journal in the field of public personnel management in the United States, and Dr. Bright has published several times in personnel journals. But their journal impact factors for the field of public administration/public management as a whole are quite low and their acceptance rate is much higher relative to top-impact journals. Likewise, JPAE is the top journal in public affairs education, but its overall journal impact factor is also small. It is not clear whether Dr. Bright deliberately targeted midlevel general journals to increase publication numbers (which is certainly a very legitimate strategy at an early stage in his career, but a dangerous one for promotion to full professor) or whether these articles were not accepted in the higher-impact general journals. Regardless, without evidence of a continuing and sustained ability to publish in high-impact journals such as PAR and JPART (and I would add Governance)- and absent a path-breaking article or a book-promotion to full professor is problematic from my perspective.

Second, the quantity of Dr. Bright's research output is problematic for promotion at top-tier universities where I have served. He has published 14 referred articles and one book chapter in 15 years. I am not suggesting that numbers alone ensure either quality of the research or the researcher, nor connote impact in the field. There are a lot of reasons why journals accept or reject articles, and some have only a tangential relationship to quality. Moreover, major leaders in our field historically have been remembered for one or two quality publications and/or for the methodological, conceptual, and/or substantive innovations they brought to field. Those (such as myself) able to added *"another brick in the wall"* make important contributions in a normal science sense. But they typically need greater numbers of high-impact journal publications and/or well reviewed books appearing consistently over the years to stand out as giving them enough scholarly heft to merit full professorship. Dr. Bright does publish consistently but averages only approximately one article per year (one might expect approximately two per year), has not published in the highest-impact general journals in the field, and has no well-reviewed books to compensate. Granted, he has held administrative posts for half his career, and that is commendable, suggests that he is a good departmental/university citizen, and that his colleagues value his administrative abilities. Administrative responsibilities, however, can also slow down publication rates. But our field is full of people who have had major administrative responsibilities and still maintained a higher rate of publication in top- and mid-tier refereed journals than has Dr. Bright.

Dr. Bright's citation counts are strong for his top-cited articles, and he should be complimented for this. However, his Google Hersch h-index (9) and i-10 (8 out of 14) index scores are rather low for promotion to full professor. Citation metrics can vary by field, so caution is needed when doing comparisons (see, for example, A W. Harzing and S. Alakangas, 2016. Google Scholar, Scopus, and the Web of Science, A longitudinal and Cross-Disciplinary Comparison, Scientometrics, 106 ,2, 787-804). That said, Hirsch finds that after 20 years of research, an h-index of 20 is generally good for researchers, 40 is outstanding, and 60 is exceptional. Meanwhile. Dr. Bright's h-10 index- meaning the number of articles cited at least 10 times-is 8 (out of 14). Dr. Bright has 15 years of service. Again, citation rates and indices such as these are tricky, and topical variation in citation rates is no doubt affecting his index scores. This is especially true given his early focus on educational issues for which much smaller bodies of research exist in public affairs compared to PSM and, thus, vastly less opportunity for citation. But, in my judgment, Dr. Bright's relatively low index number compared to Hirsch's estimates indicates that promotion to full professor is premature at this time. Third, much of Dr. Bright's research stems from two to three major surveys that, while important, suggest limitations in interpretation due to the representativeness of respondents.

Other shortcomings include under- or oversampling of particular demographics, questions regarding the actual direction of the relationships identified between or among variables, and sometimes making longitudinal inferences from cross-sectional data. Moreover, most of his work tends to treat only internal organizational variables, excluding external variables (e.g., employment opportunities when discussing turnover intent, as well as political environmental variables). In several articles related to job satisfaction and other topics, his analysis assumes that employees have control over work transfers or payments when they do not. By not asking whether employees expecting to leave a public agency seek employment in other public agencies, nonprofits, or the private sector, his measures mask whether the desire to leave reflects dissatisfaction with the public sector or not. To his credit, Dr. Bright incorporates some of the missing variables in different articles, but he does not yet combine them in one piece. Also, to his credit, he notes many of these shortcomings at the end of his article. Dr. Bright is not alone in doing these things in our field, sometimes because of the practicalities of attitude surveying and sometimes when working with existing databases that do not quite get to the real concept of interest. But, in my judgment, it takes away from the power of his findings. I hope he will follow up with these issues in future research, as he seems to have the conceptual, analytical, and theoretical skills to do so.

In sum, my reading of his research, and from my experience at other peer institutions, suggests that Dr. Leonard Bright's research record has not yet earned him promotion to full professor. But he clearly has the conceptual, analytical, and methodological skills needed to become a full professor in the future. He can· do so if he maintains an active research agenda, focuses more on targeting his PSM research to top-tier general journals with wider general audiences, and ideally publishes a well-reviewed book (which he says he is working on). His citation rate for PSM research will increase, giving him a firm position of visibility in the PSM research area, but he should also raise his general profile by assuming leadership roles in professional associations (e.g., in ASPA) and NASPAA at the national level. If you have any questions, or need clarifications, please feel free to contact me.

Reviewer 6

I am writing in response to your request that I provide a written evaluation of Professor Leonard Bright's scholarly contributions to the field and other knowledge I may have about his other professional accomplishments.

I do not know Dr. Bright. I have not come across his work in my own readings in the field. Of necessity I have approached Dr. Bright's work on public service motivation (PSM) as a first-time reader. The field has been addressing these questions about public employee attitudes for several decades. So, the topic isn't new and much foundational work has been done. (I hasten to add that this isn't a criticism; we can say this about many subject areas in Public Administration these days.) Over the past decade (or more) the work climate and public esteem of government employees have been systematically eroded, reaching what may be an all-time low at present. So, the last few years have reminded us of the importance of an experienced and public-service oriented work force to accomplish public purposes. In short, PSM has special relevance these days.

Dr. Bright has designed and collected his own data for this research. Such projects require extensive networking and consultation with target agency leadership in addition to meeting the challenges of designing, collecting, coding, and analyzing the data. He has explored the relationship of PSM to intrinsic rewards, gender differences, job satisfaction and turnover. The primary contribution of his work is to clarify the relationship of PSM to these variables. The most valuable finding is that public service motivation is more likely to result when there is a good fit between the person-organization (rather than to one's work environment or specific job). Dr. Bright has published in three Public Administration journals; the strongest is the American Review of Public Administration, which is in the top 10 according to the latest rankings I could find. His other publications in Public Administration journals are placed in specialty journals, Review of Public Personnel Administration and Public Personnel Management; both are noticeably lower on impact factor and rankings. These are considered respectable journals within their specialties.

Dr. Bright's second line of research extends his interest in public service motivation to the socialization experiences and attitudes of graduate students in public administration programs. This is an area of increasing importance to all universities. Market forces require graduate programs to be more sophisticated about identifying students with proclivities toward PSM; and once enrolled, how to nurture and sustain such motives. Bright's work identifies ways to cultivate and nurture public service motivation, through sustained and expanded students' opportunities for on-campus and off-campus experiences. In the best tradition of research informing practice, Bright's pedagogically oriented research can inform discussions about programmatic and curricular reform currently of great concern within professional associations such as NASPAA and APPAM. These research pieces provide valuable information for Public Administration programs seeking to address practical market challenges regarding recruiting and retention for Public Administration programs. These works, not surprisingly, are published in teaching-oriented journals, Teaching in Public Administration, and the Journal of Public Affairs Education (JPAE). I am familiar with JPAE. I was unable to find either of these journals listed on impact factor lists for public administration journals. Bright's publications in this arena do not extend our theoretical or conceptual understanding of PSM as a concept. Nonetheless, this work is important for administrative practice, a contribution which is often undervalued by traditional disciplines.

Your letter asked that I assess Dr. Bright's trajectory regarding his career and impact in the field. His scholarship extends the application of the well-developed PSM concept to targeted populations, local governments and graduate students. If Dr. Bright continues in this PSM vein, he would do well to research questions that are more substantive theoretically and practically.

I judge his potential career trajectory and impact for academic and/or professional leadership to be strong. My perspective is shaped by my career as a scholar and as someone who has spent many years in academic leadership positions. From my review of his CV, I anticipate that Dr. Bright's greater contribution could be in academic leadership and professional service. (I have no information on his teaching.) Research universities, with their emphasis on research and external funding, often struggle to find senior faculty members willing to go beyond the minimal service requirements (e.g., graduate admissions), unless it is a high-profile committee, perhaps something such as the President's Advisory Council. (I don't know if this is the case for the Bush School.) Dr. Bright's CV indicates extensive contributions through university, school, and departmental roles. Of course, I'm just going by what I see on his CV. You and your colleagues are the best judges of the quality and value of his contributions to the university. His service to the profession while at Texas A&M is also extensive, including American Society for Public Administration, the Southeastern Conference for Public Administration. and significant journal editorial service. 1n a way, one could say he demonstrates his own version of public service motivation; and he walks the talk.

My years in academic leadership have taught me to value faculty members who can publish and teach. and provide leadership within their academic, scholarly, and professional communities. Dr. Bright has demonstrated capable research productivity of modest impact. The strength of Dr. Bright's career trajectory may be best reflected in his contributions beyond his published research. as reflected in his significant administrative leadership roles within the university and in professional associations beyond campus.

APPENDIX E
External Reviewer Solicitation Template

At a minimum, the following language is required:

[Date]
[Name]
[Title]
[Department]
[Institution]
[Street Address]
[City, State, Zip]

Dear Professor/Dr. [Name]:

The [Unit(s)] at Texas A&M University [is/are] considering [Professor/Dr.]_____for promotion from the rank of [specify rank; specify with/without tenure] to the rank of [specify rank; specify with/without tenure]. Faculty at Texas A&M University are tenured and/or promoted on the basis of contributions in three areas: research, scholarly and creative contributions; teaching effectiveness; and service. Recognition of the quality of the candidate's scholarly work by their peers is a significant factor in the review process. We are contacting you because of your area of expertise and we value your candid assessments of [Professor/Dr.] _____scholarly accomplishments and future promise, including both areas of particular strength and areas as needing improvement. Your scholarly and professional judgement will play an important role in our evaluation of [Professor/Dr.]_____for tenure and/or promotion [specify if it is tenure only, tenure and promotion, or promotion only].

[ONLY FOR TENURE TRACK FACULTY SEEKING TENURE]: We wish to note that at Texas A&M University the

criteria for granting tenure are the same regardless of the length of a candidate's service as an untenured faculty member.

[For candidates with interdisciplinary appointments, include this paragraph:

[Candidate Name] is engaged in research that is interdisciplinary in nature. [He/she holds a joint appointment in the departments of [discipline] and [discipline]. We invite your consideration of the interdisciplinary nature of [Professor/Dr.]_____work in your review of his/her scholarly contributions]

Based on the enclosed materials and any other knowledge you have of his/her work or professional accomplishments, we would like your candid evaluation of [Professor/Dr.]_____'s written and scholarly contributions in relation to other comparable experience in their field. In particular, we would appreciate your comments on the following issues:

1. How well and in which capacity do you know [Professor/Dr.]_____?

2. Whis is your critical assessment [both strengths and areas needing improvement] of the originality, quality, and impact of [Professor/Dr.]_____'s scholarship? To facilitate your evaluation of the work in detail, I am enclosing some of [Professor/Dr.]_____'s scholarly work as well as a CV and personal statement.

3. Which if any of [Professor/Dr.]_____'scholarly publications or works do you consider to be outstanding?

4. Please describe the impact the candidate's scholarly contributions has had and/or is likely to have on the discipline.

5. What is your assessment of [Professor/Dr.]_____'s trajectory? S this faculty

member likely to become one of the leading figures in the discipline?

6. What is your overall assessment of [Professor/Dr.]_____'s standing in relation to others in their peer group who are working gin the same field?

7. Do you have any other comments that work be relevant to our deliberations, including observations about [Professor/Dr.]_____'s teaching and /or mentorship, leadership, or service?

[The following paragraph (word for word) must be included in ALL letters soliciting an evaluation of the candidate.]

Under Texas A&M University policy, your letter will become part of the official promotion packet for [Professor/Dr.]. Please note that your review will be kept confidential; however, Texas is an open records state and your review could be requested and relinquished.

It would be most helpful to receive your response by_____. I would also appreciate it if you would provide us with a short biosketch and current research interests.

We sincerely appreciate the time and effort such evaluation letters take, and thank you in advance for your important contribution to our program at Texas A&M University. If you need further information, please contact (Contact Name) at (Phone/Email).

Sincerely,

[Name][Title] Enclosures

APPENDIX F

Department and College Deliberation Memos

Department Promotion Committee Memo

The full professors on the department promotion committee (DPC) met to consider the case for Leonard Bright's promotion to full professor. Dr. Green did not attend the meeting because of her independent role as department head. Our deliberations were informed by a thorough report prepared by the evaluation subcommittee (ESC). After an examination of Leonard Bright's record and consideration of six external reviews, the committee voted unanimously that he did not merit promotion to full professor at this time.

The committee's vote as to whether Dr. Bright should be promoted to professor was 0 votes for *"yes"* and 3 votes for *"no."* All eligible members were present at the meeting and there were no abstentions or recusals.

Although more detailed assessments are available in the ESC report, the following paragraphs summarize our assessments of his record in the areas of teaching, research, and service.

Teaching

Professor Bright has taught five courses in the program since coming to the Bush School: Managing Workplace Diversity in Public and Nonprofit Organization; Public Management; Organization Theory for the Public Sector; Program Evaluation in Public and Nonprofit Organization; and Foundations of Public Service. His ability and willingness to take on a broad teaching portfolio serves important departmental needs in the area of public management. His syllabuses and other materials indicate that his courses are well-designed and rigorous, and reports based on classroom visitations by members of the ESC indicate a teaching style that is effective in conveying concepts and eliciting participation.

Student evaluations of Dr. Bright's courses are quite good except for Program Evaluation. One explanation for this anomaly may be that program evaluation is a difficult course to teach. Beyond this, the especially low scores he received were almost certainly attributable in large part to his experimental use of a grading system that relied heavily on assessments by peers as opposed to those of the professor. Although this approach may have been effective in other contexts, it was a source of confusion and led to conflict between students and the professor in program evaluation.

Research

Dr. Bright has produced fourteen journal articles as well as a chapter in an edited volume. As discussed in some detail in the ESC report and outside letters, he has pursued a coherent if somewhat narrow research agenda that has used survey data to address a series of questions with regard to public service motivation and its relationship to factors such as career choice and job satisfaction in different organizational contexts and with regard to different demographic groups. This is an area of considerable interest to students of human resources management, and his work has received more than a thousand citations. The fact that most of Professor Bright's work is single-authored also obviously leaves little doubt as to his intellectual contribution.

Having said this, the research record is thin in comparison with those of people who have been promoted to the rank of full professor at comparable institutions. Our reservations stemming from the fact that he has only fourteen peer-reviewed articles are reinforced by a consideration of where those pieces have appeared. Only one study has been published in a journal targeted to the general field of public affairs. This is the widely cited piece that appeared in the American Review of Public Administration. All the other articles are in more specialized journals devoted either to personnel administration or to pedagogical issues in public affairs. In the latter regard, five of the seven articles that Professor Bright has published since arriving at the Bush School have appeared in either Teaching Public Administration or the Journal of Public Affairs Education. These are not considered to be important outlets for research by most scholars at our peer institutions.

It was difficult securing external reviewers to assess Dr. Bright's research. Four of the people on his list declined the department's invitations and several others that he nominated did not have appropriate credentials. A number of the people initially identified by the department declined as well, but the two lists eventually yielded six well-qualified scholars to serve as reviewers identified by the department. The complete list of people who were asked to write outside letters is included in the accompanying documents. The department attempted to secure an even balance between the two lists and to avoid having letters from people affiliated with the same institution.

As noted in the ESC report, the outside letters were all carefully prepared but arrived at mixed conclusions. [Reviewers 3, 4, & 5] felt that Dr. Bright's record fell short of the criteria for promotion to full professor at a research university for the reasons we have outlined above, whereas [Reviewers 1& 2] felt that Dr. Bright's record met the bar. [Reviewer 6] indicated that Professor Bright's publication record was not strong and speculated that research might not be a priority for his career going forward. Drawing on her experience as a former Dean, however, she suggested that he might be promoted based on his willingness to contribute to the maintenance of the university as well as the public-affairs discipline through administrative activities that are important but avoided by many faculty members.

Service

Leonard Bright's record of service is in fact strong. As detailed in the ESC report, it includes participation on various departmental committees that have been responsible for important functions such as hiring, strategic planning, student recruitment, and curriculum development, among others. He has also been on a number of university-level committees and was recognized for his contributions as a member of the faculty senate. Professor Bright has also been very active outside of the university as a member of journal review boards and as a participant in professional organizations such as the American Society on Public Administration. Whether it falls under the category of service, we should also note that Dr. Bright has held administrative positions as assistant dean for Graduate Education in the Bush School and as assistant provost on the Office of Graduate and Professional Studies at Texas A&M.

Summary

In brief, Dr. Bright has more-than-satisfied expectations in the area of service and has proven to be a versatile and conscientious teacher. His recent difficulties in Program Evaluation should not persist if he is willing to restructure the course in response to student feedback. The committee's recommendation that he is not promoted to full professor at this time is based on the research record alone, and it reflects an understanding of how the department, and the Bush School have defined their missions. It is necessary to maintain high standards in this area if we are to have credibility within a tier-one research university and among our peer institutions. Although we conclude that Professor Bright is a capable scholar, his publications work in quality outlets clearly falls below the standard for promotion to full professor at the Bush School and other research-oriented schools of public affairs.

Department Head Memo

The department promotion committee (DPC) met to consider whether Leonard Bright should be promoted to the rank of full professor in the department. An evaluation subcommittee (ESC) prepared a report that helped to inform an assessment of Dr. Bright's performance. After deliberation, the committee voted 3-0 against recommending promotion. I agree with their assessment and unanimous advice, and I recommend to the dean of the Bush School that Leonard Bright not be promoted to the rank of full professor at this time.

I have satisfied myself that the committee's assessment of Dr. Bright was thorough and objective, and otherwise in accordance with our by-laws and Texas A&M regulations. The DPC chair has prepared a report that describes Dr. Bright's performance in the areas of teaching, research, and service. He vetted an earlier draft of the report with the two other committee members in order to ensure that it was factually accurate and that it captured the sense of their meeting. All three members of DPC signed the memo, conveying the report to me in my role as department head.

As noted in DPC's report, Dr. Bright is a versatile and conscientious teacher who performs at a high level. This is evidenced by the quality of his syllabi and other course materials, by his student evaluations, and by the classroom visits conducted by the members of his ESC. As department head, I greatly appreciate his willingness to teach core classes in public administration and program evaluation. He has been a particularly effective teacher in our capstone sequence. His first Capstone class represented an especially high-impact learning experience for the students, four of whom travelled to Cambodia to conduct firsthand interviews and surveys. He should be justifiably proud of the fact that the first Capstone he taught received the American Society for Public Administration (ASPA)

Appendix F

CenTex James W. McGrew Outstanding Graduate Student Research Award.

Dr. Bright's service has been exemplary. He has held significant administrative leadership roles at the college and university levels. He has served as assistant dean of Graduate Education in the Bush School and as assistant provost in the Office of Graduate and Professional Studies. He represented the Bush School on the Faculty Senate and has willingly accepted assignments to a wide variety of college- and university-level committees.

His service to the profession has been equally impressive. He currently serves on the editorial boards for two prominent journals in his field (Public Personnel Management and Review of Public Personnel Administration). He has previously served as President of the Southeastern Conference on Public Administration and has been highly active in the American Society for Public Administration (ASPA). His service to ASPA includes having served as a member of the Board of Directors for the ASPA Section on Personnel Administration and Labor Relations, and as Chair of the Strategic Imperative 4 Group. Dr. Bright received ASPA's Presidential Citation of Merit, which is presented by the ASPA president to individuals for their *"invaluable support during the presidency and tireless service to the Society."*

The committee recommendation that he is not promoted at this time is based on the research record alone. As the committee notes, over the course of his career Dr. Bright has published fourteen journal articles and one book chapter, most of which were solo authored. The committee characterized the research record as *"thin"* and expressed concern that only one of the fourteen articles (his widely piece in the American Review of Public Administration) was published in a general interest, public affairs journal. Many of the external letters also raised concerns about Dr. Bright's level of research activity. Although one letter writer noted that given the influence of his three best-cited works, Dr. Bright *"deserves to be considered as an important scholar in the study of public service motivation, and of public personnel more broadly."*

Since coming to Texas A&M as a newly promoted associate professor, Dr. Bright has published five single-authored and two co-authored articles in refereed journals. Most of these post-tenure publications (five of the seven articles) reflect his interest in the efficacy of public administration education on student career interests and have been published in either the Journal of Public Affairs Education or Teaching Public Administration. These are leading journals in the subfield of public affairs education, but they are not journals with high impact factors or high citation counts. The most-cited articles published in Teaching Public Administration in the last three years have no more than five citations each, and the most cited articles published in the Journal of Public Affairs Education have no more than 14 citations each. Although I agree with the letter writer who noted that Dr. Bright's *"recent articles are underplaced and their contribution deserves a wider readership,"* I also agree with the committee that these journals would not be considered important outlets for research by most scholars at our peer institutions. As such, I feel that Leonard Bright's scholarly record does not currently meet the threshold for promotion to full professor in the department.

Given the interdisciplinary character of our department, a key consideration in promotion and tenure decisions has been whether individuals are well-published and well-cited within their fields. This is based on the realization that different disciplines ask different questions, can value different methodological approaches, and may reflect different levels of theoretical advancement. Although his early work continues to be influential, Dr. Bright's work since coming to Texas A&M has not been as well-placed or well-received. Dr. Bright clearly satisfies the criteria for promotion with respect to teaching and service, and is a valued member of the department faculty, but I cannot support his promotion to full professor at this time.

College Promotion Committee Memo

In accordance with your charge, the college promotion committee (CPC) met to consider the case of Leonard Bright for promotion to professor.

We conducted our deliberations in accordance with the applicable sections of the Bush School and department bylaws and in conformance with university policy as stated in Rule 12.01.99.M2. As instructed, the Committee reviewed the relevant materials for Dr. Bright including the candidate's file, the external letters, the department promotion committee (DPC) votes and reports and the department head's recommendation-and used all these resources in arriving at our own independent evaluation of the case.

In terms of teaching, we agree with the DPC, and department head that Professor Bright's teaching performance and materials are good and of a quality to meet guidelines for promotion to full professor.

In terms of service, we agree with the DPC and the department head that Professor Bright's service to the department, college, University, and profession are excellent and clearly meet guidelines for promotion to full professor.

In looking at the research record, the CPC followed the department bylaws instruction that, for promotion to full professor, *"research accomplishment is demonstrated by publication of original scholarship in books and in the leading peer-reviewed journals in one's substantive field, in the fields of public or international affairs, or in relevant disciplines. Though the number of publications is taken into account, the quality and impact of publications, as demonstrated, for example, by citations and the reputation of the journals, matter more."* The department bylaws and the University Rule 12.01.99. M2. further state that the research record needs to have some measure of national recognition. These were the guiding instructions the CPC utilized in its evaluation of the case.

In our evaluations of the research case for promotion to full professor for Professor Bright we have the following observations-1) Dr. Bright has a focused and consistent research effort in the area of public management that looks into public service motivation; 2) this research has been published in a variety of journals, one highly ranked (ARPA) in terms of its breadth of influence, reputation and impact and some others that are more narrow and less tied to impactful and influential research in the broader field of public management and public policy; 3) these articles are usually single authored and based on original data gathered by Dr. Bright; 4) the total number of published articles during professor Bright's seven years here at the Bush School is 8, three of which are in fundamental public management and policy outlets and 5 of which are in more teaching of public administration outlets; 5) the quantitative impact of all of Dr. Bright's scholarship, both before and after his residency at the Bush School, as evidenced in Google Scholar statistics, is total cites= 1301, h-index = 10, and i10-index = 10.

We believe this is an adequate, but not exceptional, set of research accomplishments for an on-track, mid-level associate professor. We agree with the DPC, the department head and most of the external letters that this research record, while an acceptable one for a seven-year in-track associate professor, is not yet of a level of activity or impact that, at this time, meets the standards for a full professor in the department in the Bush School. We believe a stronger case might have been made had the request for promotion review been delayed for a few years giving more time for possible greater evidence of both scholarly activity and impact in core public administration and policy outlets.

Appendix F

At the end of its discussions, the CPC concurred with the previous levels of review and concluded that Professor Bright's case was insufficiently strong at this time to warrant promotion to full professor. The committee voted anonymously and unanimously, 0-to-4 in not recommending promotion to full professor at this time.

APPENDIX G
Dr. Bright's Post-Tenure Review Memo

This memorandum reports on the findings of the ad hoc Post-Tenure Review Committee for Associate Professor Leonard Bright. The committee consisted of three full professors who prepared the report in accordance with the department bylaws, Bush School policies, and Texas A&M University Rule on Post-Tenure Review, as detailed in System Policy 12.06.99.M2.

The committee assessed the performance of Professor Bright for the six academic years, in terms of the Standards for Post-Tenure Review, as given in Bush School Bylaws Section G.2.a-j. The committee's report is organized in terms of the customary categories for reports and reviews of tenured and tenure-track faculty members, teaching, research, and service. As specified in the Bush School Bylaws Section G.7.d, the committee relied on a compilation of the materials used by the department head to conduct annual post-tenure reviews. In addition, one member of the committee observed a class session of Professor Bright's Organizational Theory for the Public Sector course.

This report does not include an assessment of Professor Bright's activities associated with his position in the provost's office.

Dr. Bright is currently an associate professor in the department at the Bush School, and assistant provost of Graduate and Professional Studies. In the Bush School, he primarily teaches courses on public and nonprofit sector management, organization theory, workplace diversity, and program evaluation. He has been a member of the Bush School faculty at the rank of associate professor. Professor Bright served as assistant dean of graduate education at the Bush School. He assumed the position of assistant provost.

Teaching

Professor Bright's teaching load has varied because of his administrative responsibilities. We reviewed the teaching record, including student evaluations, for the courses he taught since the fall semester. He taught two courses per semester. These courses include Managing Workplace Diversity, Organizational Theory for the Public Sector, Program Evaluation for Public and Nonprofit Organizations, and Public Management.

The committee reviewed the syllabi for Professor Bright's courses, and found them to be clear, comprehensive, and well-organized. The annual review materials indicate that Professor Bright has consistently been rated as an effective instructor. His overall, course, and instructor numerical evaluation scores consistently range between 3.6 and 5.0. The one exception to this was when his scores dropped to between 2.5 and 2.9. The committee observed a class session of Professor Bright's Organizational Theory course. As noted in the report from this visit. *"Dr. Bright..follows a well-prepared class agenda and incorporates visual graphics into his lecture...[and]...has an easy, approachable teaching style...He encourages student discussion...in a very supportive and encouraging way."* Professor Bright clearly possesses extraordinary knowledge about the topics covered in the class. The committee concluded that classroom observation fully supported Professor Bright's reputation as an excellent, committed, and capable instructor.

Based on a review of all the available evidence, the committee concludes that Professor Bright's performance with respect to teaching-related criteria specified in Standards for Post-Tenure Review clearly meets the level associated with a satisfactory rating.

Research

During the review period, Professor Bright has been an active researcher and scholar. Most of his research has focused on motivations of public sector employees, and efficacy of public administration education. He published five single-author refereed journal articles, and two co-authored refereed journal articles. His articles have appeared in Public Personnel Management, Teaching Public Administration, and the Journal of Public Affairs Education. He has also presented numerous academic public administration and political science conference papers. A review of his citation record on Google Scholar reveals that his research is being read and cited. His publications have been cited some 884 times, yielding an H-Index of 7 over that period.

Based on a review of all the available evidence, the Committee concludes that Professor Bright's performance with respect to research-related criteria specified in Standards for Post-Tenure Review clearly exceeds the level associated with a satisfactory rating.

Service

With respect to service to the department and Bush School, Professor Bright has been extremely active. Service includes chairing the department's curriculum committee, and serving as a member of the department's admissions committee, and serving on three faculty search committees. He also served as a member of the McGrew Research Award Committee, as a Bush School representative to the University Faculty Senate, and as a member of the school's executive committee. As noted above, he also served as assistant dean of the Bush School for Graduate Education. Service to the profession includes chairing two committees for the American Society on Public Administration and serving as president of the Southeastern Conference for Public Administration.

The record shows that during the review period, based on a review of all the available evidence, the committee concludes that Professor Bright's performance with respect to service-related criteria specified in Standards for Post-Tenure Review exceeds the

Appendix G

level associated with a satisfactory rating. Summary The committee members unanimously concludes that the evidence showed that during the review period Professor Bright's performance meets the standard for satisfactory performance with respect to teaching, research, and service, as defined by the Standards for Post-Tenure Review (Bush School Bylaws, Section G.2.a-j).

APPENDIX H
Dr. Bright's Opening Statement to UGC

Good morning,

My name is Dr. Leonard Bright. I am an associate professor in the Department in the Bush School of Government. I want to thank the Chairman and the other members of the University Grievance Committee's Hearing Subcommittee for agreeing to conduct a detailed investigation into my allegations. The Bush School has cheated, retaliated, and discriminated against me in my application for full professor and in my recent annual review and merit salary award. Basically, I am not being held to standards that were communicated nor applied to other similarly situated faculty. Today, I will use this opportunity to provide an overview/timeline that will place my grievances into proper context.

- I joined the faculty at the Bush School as a tenured associate professor. I worked selflessly to support the research, teaching, and service expectations of my department, college, and university. After two years, I was offered a position as assistant dean by Dean Crocker. I learned early on that several faculty members in the department, including Dr. Ramsdel, disagreed with my administrative appointment. However, Dean Crocker assured me that he would support me and stand by his decision despite faculty opposition.

- The working relationship I had with Dr. Ramsdel deteriorated and resulted in him removing my wife from a teaching assignment that I believe was done in retaliation for an administrative dispute he had with me. To add insult to injury, he gave her teaching assignment to the wife of another incoming faculty member. I have supplied emails written by my wife to Dean Crocker detailing the actions Dr. Ramsdel took against her.

Appendix H

- Despite these circumstances, I served in my assistant dean role for three years. I was offered another contract to serve in this role by Dean Welsh, the current dean, upon his arrival. However, I decided to accept a two-year appointment in the Office of Graduate Studies to serve as an assistant provost.

- While serving in my college and university-level administrative roles, I maintained high productivity in research, teaching, and service, as evidenced by the very positive stances the department took toward my journal quality, research impact, and publication numbers. At no point did the department conclude that my research performance did not, at the very least, meet its expectations. This is important because Texas A&M's policy 12.01.99.M2 University Statement on Academic Freedom, Responsibility, Tenure, and Promotion, Section 2.4.1 states.

    "The purpose of the annual review is to provide a mechanism to facilitate dialogue between the administration and faculty. The annual review provides the process to evaluate the faculty members' accomplishments in the context of departmental, college and university goals. Annual reviews are to be conducted in an environment of openness and collegiality, with an emphasis on constructive development of the individual faculty member and the institution."

- As a matter of fact, in the Post Tenure Report, an ad hoc 3- member committee of department full professors concluded.

    "Based on a review of all the available evidence, the Committee concludes that Professor Bright's performance with respect to research-related criteria specified in Standards for Post-Tenure Review clearly exceeds the level associated with a satisfactory rating."

Specifically, Texas A&M's policy 12.06.99. M0.01 Post-Tenure Review, Section 3.1 states,

> "The purpose of the Periodic Peer Review is to assess whether the individual is making a contribution consistent with that expected of a tenured faculty member, provide guidance for continuing and meaningful faculty development; assist faculty to enhance professional skills and goals, and refocus academic and professional efforts, when appropriate."

Even more, it is important to note that I served under three different department heads and three deans over this seven-year period. Again, at no point did these leaders criticize my research accomplishments, but instead applauded my research and encouraged it to continue.

- I applied for promotion to full professor. Dr. Ramsdel was appointed to serve as the chair of my promotion process, even though he had indicated in an earlier meeting that he would recuse himself. When I became aware that he had assumed the leadership role over my promotion process, I complained to the outgoing interim department head #3. He assured me that he would discuss the matter with the dean's office. In the meantime, while I waited for Dr. Ramsdel's replacement, I attempted to work with him to complete the selection of the external reviewers. Unfortunately, Dr. Johnson (interim department head) never followed up with me regarding my concerns about Dr. Ramsdel's involvement.

- I strongly contented with Dr. Ramsdel's overt efforts to reject my external reviewer choices. During several email exchanges, Dr. Ramsdel repeatedly encouraged me to be *"strategic"* by *"leaving some people off"* of my external reviewer list who *"would provide favorable reviews."* I did not comply with his request.

- Dr. Green informed me that a three-member department faculty committee voted against my application and that 4 of 6 of my external letters were not supportive. When

Appendix H

I asked for the reasons for the decision, she stated that it was for low research performance and that he resonated with a *"rule of thumb"* assessment offered by one of the reviewers who stated that a google scholar H index of 20 and 20+ published works are the standards for full promotion. She then followed this up with an assessment that my scholarly impacts were more consistent with the standards for promotion to associate professor, rather than to full professor. I told her that these were not standards applied to other similarly situated faculty in the department and that I took her statements to be an insult. As the conversation concluded, Dr. Green insisted twice that I withdraw my promotion application. When I refused, she stated that my decision was *"a mistake"* which I understood to be a threat.

- I filed a written formal complaint with Dean Welsh that described my conversation with Dr. Green and my allegations of cheating, discrimination, and retaliation that I believed I was experiencing in the promotion process based on the information he provided. In subsequent emails, I provided additional contextual clarifications regarding my contentious relationship with Dr. Ramsdel, the links between the Year 6 salary disparity I experienced and my allegations of retaliation, etc.

- I filed a formal complaint with the EEOC.

- I continued to describe the situation as I understood it at the time, asked that the CPC be made aware of the situation, and attempted to schedule a meeting with Dean Welsh, with my spouse present.

- I was finally able to meet face to face with Dean Welsh. However, during the meeting he largely dismissed my complaints, blamed me for not notifying the department of my complaints sooner, and defended the DPC chair's actions. He also informed me that Dr. Ramsdel had gained approval from the Dean of Faculties (DOF) to remain the chair of my promotion process, in full knowledge of our contentious relationship. Immediately after the meeting, I made the provost aware of the situation. Dean Welsh then attempted to refute my description of the meeting, after which I provided him with direct quotes. The provost asked that I forward my discrimination complaints to OREC.

- In a meeting with the DOF, I was informed that my promotion process had been stopped. The DOF also strongly denied Dean Welsh's statement regarding Dr. Ramsdel gaining approval to remain the chair of my promotion process and they promised to follow-up with me after an internal investigation into the matter, which they did not do.

- The EEOC provided me with the department's promotion committee recommendation letter written which contained evidence that non-independent external reviewers were used (i.e., former co-workers and co-authors were used and not acknowledged as such in the letter) as well as other serious violation of Texas A&M's written promotion guidelines which I outlined in my grievance to the UGC.

- I notified the provost of my discoveries in a good faith effort to resolve my case. However, my attempts at resolution were largely ignored and my questions went unanswered, even when I directly asked the provost for a response.

- I received Dr. Green's Year 8 annual review. In stark difference from prior annual evaluations, Dr. Green criticized both my current and past research accomplishments, applied evaluation ratings that were not defined in the department bylaws, issued threats regarding my future service accomplishments, offered conclusions that directly contradicted precedent set by the Bush School in all previous annual reviews over the past seven years, and determined that my research activities were now in need of improvement. Even though Dean Welsh rescinded her annual evaluation and required her to increase her assessment to *"satisfactory,"* Dr. Green evaluation continued to assert standards that are not defined in the department bylaws, and failed to clearly explained why her conclusions contradict the precedent set by the Bush School in all previous annual reviews over the past seven years.

- Similarly, when I asked how this improved evaluation would affect my merit increase, Dr. Green disclosed an incomplete merit evaluation system that she claims she used. Despite my repeated requests, the department and the Bush School refused to provide the standards and benchmarks that were used in their merit/salary decisions to judge my research and teaching accomplishments.

- Dean Welsh notified me that Texas A&M was restarting my promotion process and that he had recused himself. He also noted that another college dean was selected by provost to serve as the dean reviewer.

- I met with Dean Welsh to hear the reasons for his recusal, since he would not provide them in writing. Basically, he indicated that he recused himself because he was angry with me. That same day, I emailed the provost with a summary of the meeting, expressed my displeasure with his statements, and requested that an alternative dean be assigned for all evaluative matters concerning me. The DOF briefly responded that *"Dean Welsh should not recuse himself from any administrative decision-making processes associated with me..."*

- I decided to send a formal grievance to the UGC regarding the promotion process that was used by the Bush School and the treatment I experienced.

- I was informed by the DOF that the president had denied my promotion application, which was the only update I have received since meeting with Dean Welsh. This contradicts the DOF promotion guidelines, which required a progress update at each level of the decision-making process.

In conclusion, I am appalled by the treatment I have received in the Bush School. I have experienced multiple irregularities of flagrant, cheating, discrimination, and retaliation during my promotion review and Year 8 annual review, though the UGC is not charged with investigating my discrimination claims. Sadly, my experiences at Texas A&M are typical of how many Black faculty are treated in traditionally white universities and departments. I am the only tenured Black faculty at the Bush School, and it should not be lost on anyone that it has never hired or promoted a Black faculty to the rank of full professor in its entire history. So, to be clear, the problems I face have nothing to do with my failure to meet the expectations of my department. The department has consistently and repeatedly communicated that I met and exceeded their expectations in research, teaching, and service in all past reviews. The problem is that the department has now decided not to apply the standards that they communicated to me because they do not prefer the administrative roles I have been granted, my race, as well as my audacity to speak up and demand fair treatment. Even more, I allege that they engaged in an effort to rig my full promotion process by selecting and encouraging their friends to provide information they could use to contradict the department's previous evaluations and infect my future evaluations. If the Aggie Code is more than a slogan, these practices should not be tolerated nor excused.

It is up to Texas A&M to enforce its Aggie codes, bylaws, policies, expectations, and standards as communicated, as well as the laws of the land that prohibit discrimination and retaliation.

Chairman and other members of the UGC's Hearing Subcommittee, I want to thank you for this opportunity and look forward to your questions.

APPENDIX I

Ad Hoc Committee Memo on Dr. Bright Salary Grievance Investigation

The Interim DOF appointed an ad hoc committee, consisting of senior professors from three colleges, in accordance with System Rule SAP 12.99.99.M0.01 (Faculty Grievance Procedures Not Concerning Questions of Tenure, Dismissal or Constitutional Rights), to consider the salary grievance of Dr. Leonard Bright (Bush School). The ad hoc committee received and reviewed Dr. Bright's written complaint. The ad hoc committee met (via Zoom) with Dr. Bright to discuss his complaint. The ad hoc committee requested via the Interim DOF additional information relating to salaries and evaluations at the Bush School. That additional information was received by the committee. The committee then reviewed that information, met twice via Zoom, and provided the following report.

The Bush School's assessment of Dr. Bright's salary is based on his annual evaluations and comparisons with others in his field and other related fields. However, our committee finds several problems and inconsistencies in the assessment. In what follows, we examine the complaint from two angles: (i) salary comparisons with people with same degrees (ii) annual evaluations in the PSAA department.

Salary Comparisons

The main arguments advanced by [Dean Mark Welsh] Bush School's Dean of the salary disparity rest on comparison of salaries of professor at the Bush school with salaries of professors with same degrees at other schools and departments. There are two very different ways the PSAA department arrives at these comparisons, and in what follows, we examine both.

Appendix I

Salary of "Political Scientists"

The Bush School's Dean states that Dr. Bright's salary is above his peers in the Political Science Department at Texas A&M University:

> *"In fact, according to the DOF salary survey data, Dr. Bright would have been the second highest paid associate professor in the TAMU Department of Political Science at that time."*

But Dr. Bright is not a political scientist. His Ph.D. is in public administration. He can be compared with others with a similar degree. Equity demands that we compare him with other public administration scholars and political scientists within the Bush School (rather than the TAMU Political Science Department), and on such examination, his salary seems low. Before his adjustment in [Year 4], his monthly salary was [omitted]. In the same year, Dr. [Faculty 1], an assistant professor in the PSAA Department with a similar public administration degree, received $11,666.67 per month. Even though Dr. Bright had arrived at the Bush School with tenure eight years earlier in [Year 8], his monthly salary was only $719.39 higher than Dr. [Faculty 1]'s. Fortunately, Dr. Bright's salary was adjusted in [Year 4] when he received a 14.38% equity raise. Even so, Dr. Bright's salary was [omitted] (per month), while Dr. [Faculty 1]'s salary was [omitted]. As of [Year 3] Dr. [Faculty 1] has been promoted to associate professor with tenure. That year, Dr. [Faculty 1] earned a monthly salary of [omitted] as compared to Dr. Bright's [omitted]. This year [Year 7] Dr. [Faculty 1] earns [omitted] as compared to Dr. Bright's [omitted] per month. Dr. Bright's monthly salary is just $1,023 more than Dr. [Faculty 1]'s, even though the former was tenured nine years earlier than the latter. Even though Dr. Bright's salary increase during [Year 5-2] kept pace with Dr. [Faculty 1]'s, his current salary still seems to be lower than what his experience and research impact warrants. It is pertinent to note that as of [Year 8],

Dr. [Faculty 1] has 222 citations as compared to Dr. Bright's 2,137 citations (Google Scholar).

Comparing Dr. Bright's salary to other political scientists within the Bush School shows a similar pattern. Dr. [Faculty 2], a political scientist at the Bush School's INTA department, was tenured in Year 8], four years after Dr. Bright. According to the table on p. 52, his monthly salary is [omitted], which puts him a touch below Dr. Bright. Dr. [Faculty 2]'s higher salary does not seem to reflect greater research productivity. Dr. [Faculty 2] has had only 352 citations, which is significantly lower than Dr. Bright's 2,137

Salary of "Economists"

The incomplete note by Dean Welsh advances a claim that the economists should be paid higher than non-economists. This assertion is highly problematic and has led to several inconsistencies in salaries within the Bush school itself. The Bush School has six economists: four in the PSAA department and two in the INTA department. It is unclear why the four economists in the PSAA department have received disproportionately large raises. Dr. [Faculty 3] and Dr. [Faculty 4], the two economists in the INTA department, do not appear to have received the same salary adjustments.

Dr. [Faculty 3]'s salary is substantially below that of fellow economist associate professors in the PSAA department. The Dean states that she received a 7 percent adjustment in [Year 6]. But this only brought her closer to her economist colleagues in the PSAA department before they received their major salary raises in the following year. Currently, Dr. [Faculty 3]'s monthly salary is [omitted] which is below that of her peers, Dr. [Faculty 5], and Dr. [Faculty 6]. Dr. [Faculty 5] and Dr. [Faculty 6] received their tenure a year before and two years after Dr. [Faculty 3], respectively. Dr. [Faculty 3]'s salary is currently on par with Dr. [Faculty 7]'s, but the latter was tenured 5 years after Dr. [Faculty 3]. Dr. [Faculty 7] has only 449 citations, while Dr. [Faculty 3] has 2,034. Dr. [Faculty 4]'s salary has not changed significantly in recent years. In fact, his salary is lower than that of all the other full professors in the INTA department (all of whom are political scientists). Clearly, the idea of higher pay for economists (regardless of the fairness and equity concerns) has not even been implemented equally at the Bush School between the two departments.

Applying the lens of equity and fairness, the justification for different salaries for the economists rests on an unproven assumption that such is necessary for retention in all cases (except Dr. [Faculty 3]'s where "there was no external hiring pressure."). It is one thing to raise an individual's salary based on an actual offer, it is a very different thing to have a blanket rule for all cases in one of the School's departments wherein there may or may not be external hiring pressure.

Case-by-case decision-making may justify some differentiation, but there is little justification for instituting a rule that sweeps in like and unalike individuals. Further, the justification for treating all economists differently because they are economists appears pretextual in the light of the exclusion of Dr. [Faculty 3] from that blanket rule. Her salary is set after a case-by-case determination of a lack of external hiring pressure, but other economists in the PSAA department get the benefit of the blanket rule.

Overall, salary increases deployed in the Bush School based on Dean Welsh' arguments appear to be problematic. If economists choose to join the Bush school, they should accept the prevailing salary structures within the ranges of equity, and neither demand nor expect special pay packets based on their doctoral degrees. The same goes with scholars with political science or public administration degrees.

Annual Evaluations at the PSAA Department

This committee's second concern derives from the annual evaluations deployed at the PSAA department, which, in part, guides the salary increases. It appears that the PSAA Department has not assessed Dr. Bright's publication outlets clearly or consistently.

Dr. Bight's evaluation reports in [Year 6] and [Year 5] expressed no concerns over the quality of journals that Dr. Bright chooses to publish in. The then Department Head (DH) and the acting DH at the time praised him for publishing in these journals:

> *"During the review period, you had a most successful and productive year with respect to research. A co-authored article with Blease Graham appeared in print in the Journal of Public Affairs Education. Two additional sole-authored articles were published during the review period—one in Public Personnel Management and another in Teaching Public Administration. In addition, you have another forthcoming article to appear in Teaching Public Administration and yet another under review in Public Personnel Management. This is an excellent record of productive scholarly achievement."*

However, the [Year 4] letter to Dr. Leonard Bright from Dr. Green differs markedly from the letters issued in [Year 6] and [Year 5] to Dr. Bright in tone, tenor, and assessment. In the [Year 4] evaluation, the new DH [Dr. Green] expressed concerns that Dr. Bright's articles had not appeared in high impact journals:

"I would like to raise concerns with you regarding your choice of research outlets. Much of your recent work has been published in either the Journal of Public Affairs Education or Teaching Public Administration. I recognize that you may consider these the leading journals in the subfield of public affairs education, but these are not journals with high impact factors or high citation counts. The most-cited article published in Teaching Public

Appendix I

Administration in the last three years has no more than five citations, and the most-cited article published in the Journal of Public Affairs Education has only 13 citations. I believe that your recent articles were under-placed and their contribution deserved a wider readership."

However, a quick look at Dr. Bright's Google Scholar account shows that the new DH's estimate of the impact of his articles in these journals may have been incorrect. As of [Year 1], his [Year 5], [Year 6], and [Year 7] articles in Teaching Public Administration have had 11, 3, and 22 citations, respectively. Meanwhile his [Year 7] and [Year 8] articles in the Journal of Public Affairs Education have received 19 and 33 citations, respectively.

This changing pattern of evaluation appears problematic. Additionally, based on the limited information that we have, the scoring systems that the PSAA DH has adopted seem unclear and inconsistent. In one year, Dr. Bright received "6" for research which was similar to or higher than most other tenured professors in his department. But in the next year, he received the lowest possible score of "1" which was below the entire department, even the practitioner faculty who have no research obligations. This is when Dr. Bright is the most cited associate professor in the entire Bush School.

Overall, this committee finds merit in the complaint advanced by Dr. Leonard Bright that there is a salary discrepancy that exists in the PSAA department which does not stand the scrutiny of equity, merit, and consistency in evaluation.

APPENDIX J

DOF Memo about Dr. Bright Salary Equity Raise

From: Interim DOF
To: Dean Welsh and Provost

Dr. Leonard Bright, associate professor in the Department of Public Service and Administration in the Bush School of Government and Public Service, submitted a salary grievance to the Dean of Faculties Office citing University Rule 12.99.99. M0.01. The rationale for the grievance was his unequal pay compared to other associate professors in the department and college, without consideration of time in rank and productivity. Dr. Bright met with his department head to discuss his salary correction request. Following a negative recommendation from his department head, Dr. Bright appealed for a dean-level review, which in upheld the decision of the department head. Dr. Bright appealed to the Dean of Faculties who appointed an ad hoc committee to evaluate the case in accordance with section 8.1 of University Rule 12.99.99. M0.01. Per section 8.2 of the same rule, the Dr. Bright was given the opportunity to evaluate the nominations of potential members of the ad hoc committee and approved all three members who formed the committee.

1. After reading Dr. Bright's written statement and hearing from him directly, the ad hoc committee decided that the grievance merited a detailed investigation. They then submitted a request for the following materials from the Bush School of Government & Public Service to support their investigation:
2. Year-to-year 9-month and total salary details for all associate professors in the Department of Public Service and Administration (PSAA), from [Year 11] onwards.
3. Performance evaluations from [Year 6] onwards for all associate professors in the PSAA department at Bush School of Government & Public Service. The request included all comments made by all the people who were involved in the review of associate professors.

Appendix J

4. A detailed rationale for the salary adjustment of economists vs. non-economists (or earlier or later) in the PSAA department at Bush School of Government & Public Service.
5. The salary structure in the two departments within the Bush School of Government & Public Service. Specifically requested were, (a) if the Department of International Affairs (INTA) applies the same policy of basing the salary on degree level of faculty and (b) The salary details of the economist and non-economist faculty who are on the same level for the past three years in INTA (assistant/associate/full).
6. Percentage increases in salary for all faculty (assistant/associate/full) in the PSAA department, and the detailed rationale.

The Bush School of Government & Public Service delivered all the requested information. After reviewing the documents, the ad hoc committee provided their report and recommendation to Dean of Faculties. The report was also shared with the grievant in accordance with section 8.2.2 of university rule 12.99.99.M0.01.

The ad hoc committee found merit in the complaint advanced by Dr. Bright in that there exists a salary discrepancy in the PSAA department. I concur with this assessment and provide a justification for a salary correction below. For context, and to support my analysis of the case, I used the following guiding principles considered for evaluating salary corrections:

1. Recommendations for faculty equity adjustments should consider a variety of individual faculty characteristics including:

    a. Years in rank.

    b. Performance / productivity in key domains associated with professorial rank, e.g. for tenure-track and tenured (TT) faculty: research scholarship and teaching, and for academic professional track (APT) faculty: teaching and program development. Service/professional engagement may also be considered but to a lesser extent.

c. Performance-based equity adjustments should not be based on one-year's performance; this should be reflected in merit adjustments. A performance-based equity adjustment should rather be based on multi-year demonstration of productivity. As such, a high performance noted in a recent annual merit evaluation should be a necessary, but not sufficient condition for consideration of an equity adjustment.

d. Within key domains of faculty productivity, (e.g., research scholarship, teaching, and program development) specific areas of performance that are aligned with the unit (e.g. department or college) strategic and aspirational goals will be heavily weighted in equity decisions (e.g., grants and contract activity, recruitment and retention of historically under-represented students, development and implementation of high impact and technology-mediated instructional activities, types of degree managed, mentorship of graduate students with appropriate time to degree).

2. Both salary comparison information from discipline-based analyses and nested within peer institutions and salary compression/inversion information within TAMU academic units may be considered as part of the rationale for equity adjustments; however, they should be secondary to performance/productivity indicators.

Based on the review of the ad hoc committee, the information provided by the Bush School of Government & Public Service,

Appendix J

and the guiding principles listed above, I provide below my recommendation on the salary grievance by Dr. Leonard Bright:

1. As indicated in guiding principle #2 above, academic units can set salary structures based on well established, and consistently applied market analyses (peer institutions) of professional remuneration. In that context, it is appropriate to remunerate faculty with economics degrees at a premium as is often the practice across institutions of higher education in the U.S. However, that process must be performed consistently across all positions and in accordance with guiding principle #1 (time in rank, productivity, alignment with strategic initiatives). The Bush School of Government & Public Service can thus remunerate its economics faculty at a premium but should do so applying the principle equitably across all departments and faculty ranks. The lower remuneration of Drs. [Faculty 3 and Faculty 4] are problematic in that context of premium remuneration, especially since both are notably productive faculty. I recommend that the Dean of the Bush School of Government & Public Service evaluate the salary structure of the economics faculty and develop a set of principles such as presented above to define what the premium remuneration should be for each at their respective rank, years in rank, and level of productivity. This evaluation may result in correction for some of their economics faculty.

2. Dr. Bright is a productive faculty based on his number of publications over time, as well as his consistent and high-citation report. Similarly, his service and teaching impact have met expectations repeatedly except for the hiatus year. Following his [recent] evaluation, Dr. Bright increased his productivity and impact in all dimensions and again met expectations. Hence, when his salary is compared to other associate professors in areas not in economics (i.e.., Drs Faculty 1 and Faculty 2), his time

and rank and most importantly his productivity are not recognized appropriately.

Based on this analysis, I recommend that Dr. Bright's salary be adjusted upwards to recognize his time in rank and consistent productivity across the years. Both elements should be sufficient to justify moving him into the range of the three economics faculty in his department while still honoring the principle of developing and supporting a discipline-based salary structure (all three have less time in rank and cumulative productivity is lower or comparable).

I am available were you to have any questions

.

APPENDIX K
Dr. Bright's Open Letter to University Community

Considering the news that Acting President Welsh will attend a meeting with the Executive Committee of the Faculty Senate and the full Senate, I have decided to provide a letter regarding my experiences at Texas A&M University (TAMU), under Mark Welsh, in the Bush School of Government.

I joined the faculty in the Bush School as a tenured associate professor 12 years ago. I am the only tenured Black faculty in my department, and one of two in the entire college. Four years ago, I went through a discriminatory full professor promotion process whereby then Dean Mark Welsh was made aware that my colleagues had violated TAMU's written guidelines, did not use the promotion standards applied to my peers, and instead obtained non-independent external review letters from 5 reviewers they selected who were their ex-Bush School employees, and/or their co-authors and close friends. Through discovery and open record requests, I obtained email communications between the chair of my promotion process and several external reviewers, which suggested that he readily engaged in off-the-record conversations with potential reviewers, communicated his disagreement with my decision to apply for promotion, and made false claims about my performance at TAMU.

As dean, Mark Welsh did not correct the situation when he was made aware of it, but instead he immediately retaliated against me when he learned that I had filed an Employment Opportunity Commission (EEOC) complaint by recusing/abandoning the promotion process. I was the only case to ever come out of the Bush School without a Dean's review. I was also subjected to retaliation in my annual reviews by my department head (Dr. Green) immediately after my EEOC complaint, one of which was so bad that the university decided to rescind it. He suffered no apparent penalty by Dean Welsh for his actions.

I appealed to the 2020 University Grievance Committee (UGC) who agreed to investigate my treatment in the promotion process and subsequent annual reviews. During an open recorded hearing, Dean Welsh slandered my character by describing me as *"aggressive, not civil, bullying, not fit for the field of public service...etc."* Several members of the UGC rebuked him and noted that his comments were racially charged, deeply troubling, and routinely assigned to blacks who are seeking fair treatment. After this committee concluded their investigation and issued their report to the provost, the provost decided to remove his supervisory responsibility over me for two years. However, to this day, TAMU and Faculty Affairs refuse to provide me with the UGC's final report issued to the provost. I was finally promoted to full professor to be effective this September 1st, but even after this hard fight, I still have had to file multiple internal grievances and another EEOC complaint to address the salary disparities, and the denial of endowed professorships, and research support that all of my peer colleagues have received.

Consistent with what Dr. Kathleen McElroy experienced, as a Black faculty at TAMU, I have also received greater scrutiny in the promotion process, annual review process, and denied other benefits that I have earned. I am forced to endure a culture that ignores the pervasive barriers placed in my pathway. Only after years of enduring and fighting such poor treatment was I finally able to receive a measure of what some of my peers easily receive for the same or lower performance. TAMU has defended their treatment of me under the guise of what it calls *"academic determination,"* to shield itself from external accountability. Their defense minimizes the fact that no faculty (including Black Faculty) should endure such poor treatment to obtain what we have earned.

So, we all should know the specifics of what Acting President Mark Welsh will do to fix the poor treatment which occurred during the Kathleen McElroy and Joy Alonzo controversies, especially given his own treatment of his own Black faculty in the Bush School. Acting President Welsh is exceptionally good at making glowing public statements of support for one issue or another. TAMU faculty, staff, and students deserve much better than mere words. We deserve better treatment.

Dr. Leonard Bright

APPENDIX L
Final UGC Report

Scope of the allegations

The allegations that were the content of this grievance were provided to the DOF in two documents. They contained allegations of cheating related to the conduct of the evaluation of Dr. Bright, for promotion from associate professor to full professor, which resulted in denial of promotion.

General/historical Background

The department in the Bush School of Government is a relatively small department, in a small college, with few tenured professors, including both associate and full professors. The lack of critical mass means that faculty are called upon to play multiple 'gatekeeper' roles in areas of promotion and tenure, that at times gives the appearance of conflict of interest. There is also a lack of diversity in the faculty body (acknowledged by Dean Welsh), which may result in the emergence of a cultural 'groupthink' that disfavors culturally non- aligned minorities. In this context, Dr. Bright, the sole African American tenured faculty member, has the appearance of a social isolate within this department

The grievant, Dr. Bright, was hired as an associate professor with tenure. He is the sole tenured African- American faculty member in that department or college. All other faculty who are persons of color are non-tenured. One other tenured professor, who was a person of color, left A&M previously. During Dr. Bright's tenure at A&M, the Bush School was headed by 3 deans. There were also 4 different department heads (one served at two different points in time, once as interim head), including Dr. Ramsdel, who served as interim head. The current department head, Dr. Green assumed the position of department head.

Appendix L

At the time of his hire, Dr. Bright's spouse was also hired in a part-time teaching role.

During Dr. Ramsdel's tenure as interim department head, Dr. Bright was also appointed to the position of Vice-dean of Graduate Education. The letters provided by Dr. Bright clearly show that the leadership of the Bush School valued his service in that position. However, it is disquieting to note that Dr. Ramsdel characterized the position of vice-dean as undesirable and not a job that anyone would want to do (this point will be brought up later). Dr. Ramsdel also resisted Dr. Bright's apparently legitimate requests, in his capacity as vice-dean for graduate education, for information about students in the 3+2 program. Shortly after that conflict over administrative responsibilities, Dr. Ramsdel terminated the appointment of Dr. Bright's spouse. Dr. Ramsdel maintained, when interviewed as a fact witness, that he was within his rights to terminate the appointment of Dr. Bright's spouse with no explanation, due to her position as an adjunct. However, he did proffer an explanation to the GRC, that the teaching position was needed for someone else. It is also disquieting to note that Dr. Ramsdel characterized Dr. Bright as a liar, suggesting a high level of antipathy (in fairness, it appears that Drs. Ramsdel and Bright have a mutual sense of antipathy, though Dr. Ramsdel's position as chair of the promotions committee lends power asymmetry to such antipathy). These instances of conflict may be coincidental and innocuous but may equally point to the existence of a toxic and retaliatory culture. However, they do provide context for Dr. Bright's grievance.

Dr. Bright moved from his role as assistant dean at the Bush School, to the role of assistant provost for Graduate Studies at TAMU. His annual reviews suggested that he was effective and valued in this new role. Moreover, the testimony of the Dean of Faculties indicates that he was personable, friendly, and professional in this role (this is a point that will be brought up later, because it contrasts with characterizations of Dr. Bright's behavior by Dean Welsh).

During this period, Dr. Bright received uniformly positive annual review evaluations for his teaching, research, and service. He also successfully passed his post-tenure review.

Dr. Bright stepped down from his role as assistant provost to return to full-time duties in the department. His full-time commitment to the department, as outlined in his annual review letter was divided as follows, 60% effort towards teaching, 30% effort towards research and 10% effort towards service. At this time, Dr. Bright also initiated a request for promotion to professor and subsequently received the first obviously adverse annual review from the newly appointed department head, Dr. Green.

Grievance: Allegations of cheating related to the conduct of the evaluation of Dr. Bright, for promotion from associate professor to full professor

Issue #1: Recusal of Dr. Ramsdel from the review process.

This report outlines a history of conflict between the grievant and Dr. Ramsdel. Dr. Ramsdel claims that he sought advice on his potential recusal from Dr. Bright's promotions committee, from the dean of Faculty's office. He indicated that a [name omitted] told him over the phone that it would be acceptable for him to serve as chair of Dr. Bright's promotions committee. However, the DOF's testimony did not support Dr. Ramsdel's version of events. According to the DOF would never have given such advice but would have referred the requestor to the DOF for further consultation. Moreover, the DOF outlined what is a well-accepted standard, that, 'if an individual feels that they are in conflict, then they should recuse themselves.' The appearance of conflict of interest matters and is enough grounds for recusal.

Finding: The GRC finds that Dr. Ramsdel should have recused himself from chairing Dr. Bright's promotions committee. It is highly probable that his continued participation contaminated the promotions process.

Recommendations: The GRC recommends (a) That the DOF provide written instructions for standards for recusal when a request is made. (b) Train and require staff to maintain written records of inquiries (whether initiated verbally or otherwise) by responding via e-mail to all such inquiries with a summary of the discussion/recommendation, and (c) document the outcome of these inquiries and include them with a candidate's promotion files.

Issue #2: Inappropriate selection of non 'arms-length' referees and inappropriate elimination of referees from Dr. Bright's list.

The grievant, respondents and one fact witness (Dr. Ramsdel) all agree that a majority of referees from Dr. Bright's list were eliminated and that multiple referees from the same institution were solicited and responded. It is also not disputed that some of these referees were former Texas A&M faculty who were known to and associated with Bush School faculty. The position of Dr. Ramsdel was that Dr. Bright's list was comprised of referees who (a) were unacceptable because they did not come from peer institutions or (b) declined to provide a letter. In response to these concerns being raised, Dr. Bright did provide an expanded list of referees, but these were not fully utilized either. As chair of Dr. Bright's promotion committee, Dr. Ramsdel, in his oral testimony, attributed their difficulty with finding willing referees to Dr. Bright's failure to achieve a sufficiently high research reputation.

However, the testimony of Dr. Ramsdel is contradicted by testimony provided by the DOF. The DOF indicated that across the entire Texas A&M University, promotions committees are finding it increasingly difficult to obtain referee letters, and that if the promotions committee does not act early, it is likely to meet with rejection from over- committed referees. In other words, there is a significant probability that the failure of the promotions committee to obtain letters is not a negative reflection on Dr. Bright, despite testimony to the contrary.

Given the documented perception of conflict of interest outlined above, the fairness of referees who were former Texas A&M faculty colleagues or members of the Bush School is also questionable. GRC members expressed discomfort with what was felt to be an inappropriate degree of proximity between referees and Bush School faculty. It cannot be definitely determined that their referee letters were not also contaminated by their association with, and proximity to a perceived conflict of interest. Therefore, caution must be exercised in interpreting those letters

The DOF also testified that the goal, to obtain referee letters from peer institutions, was aspirational, but that many promotions committees across A&M have petitioned, and received permission, to utilize people at institutions that fell outside those guidelines. The DOF did not recollect the department promotion committee (DPC) making such a request. According to Dr. Ramsdel's testimony such a request was not considered for any of the people on Dr. Bright's list. At the very least, this indicates a lack of support and effort to request and obtain as many letters as needed/possible for Dr. Bright's promotion case. At worst it may indicate a concerted effort to derail the case for Dr. Bright's promotion. Regardless, such inaction emphasizes the view from the outside that Dr. Bright was an isolated member of this department

The standards applied to Dr. Bright are likely to have a disparate impact, because of his race. As indicated in this report, the value of Dr. Bright's promotions package was inappropriately diminished because of the inability of the committee to find referees. Complicating the already documented difficulties with finding referees across TAMU, are the special circumstances surrounding faculty of color. Underrepresented minority (URM) faculty have been reported to have smaller co-author networks and the reach of these networks is also smaller, which is likely to be a significant barrier to reputational advancement. URM faculty are also more likely to experience isolation, lack of mentoring and disrespect. Not surprisingly, these structural impediments within institutions can have significant consequences for future success. For example, an analysis of applications for grant funding from the National Institutes of Health showed that Black faculty applicants had fewer publications, with fewer citations and that these citations were in lower impact factor journals than white applicants. These differences explained 52% of the black/white funding gap for NIH grant funding. Further, even after controlling for publication record, black faculty are 10 percentage points less likely than white faculty, to receive NIH funding, suggesting that black faculty disproportionately experience structural and systemic impediments to success. It has been shown that URMs, and particularly black faculty have decreased support networks, experience institutional isolation, are less likely to be at top 100 funding institutions and have to contend with significant systemic barriers to success. Consequently, URM faculty are less likely to be promoted than white faculty. To wit, in the case of Dr. Bright, the selection of *"appropriate"* letter writers without requesting special provision and/or formal guidance from the DOF office likely put his promotion case at an unfair disadvantage

Greater social capital within his small unit (including the recusal of Dr. Ramsdel from chairing the committee) might have led the promotions committee to take a more holistic view at whether the referees he listed had made significant contributions to the field versus simply dismissing them for not being at *"peer/aspirational"* institutions. It seems in this instance, that standards and perceptions for what constitutes 'appropriate referees' may have had a disproportionately adverse impact on faculty of color. In this relatively homogenous Bush School, it is therefore greatly concerning that respondents and fact witness appeared to not comprehend concepts like disparate impact.

Findings: The GRC finds that the process of referee recruitment was flawed, possibly contaminated by conflicts of interest, inappropriate interpretation, and, at least with respect to Dr. Bright, did not adequately utilize the flexibility offered by the DOF, and likely resulted in a disparately adverse impact. Statements like, *"it was difficult securing external reviewers to assess Dr. Bright's researc*h*"* are indeed prejudicial, and in the GRC's opinion, the initiating sentiment behind that statement unacceptably contaminated the review process

Recommendations: The GRC recommends that the DOF provide guidance to promotions committees and candidates (so that they may advocate for themselves) on (a) potential flexibility in the standards and rules for seeking referee letters and (b) training in implicit bias and disparate impact.

Issue #3: Inappropriate recusal of Dean Welsh and appointment of an alternate dean to oversee Dr. Bright's promotions process

As outlined above, *"The appearance of conflict-of-interest matters and is enough grounds for recusal."* Though there may not be a formal mechanism, the actions of Dean Welsh in this case are judged to be correct. If he felt that there was a conflict of interest, then he had an obligation to recuse himself, and it was well that he did so. Moreover, the DOF testified that the alternate Dean had been chosen with some attention to fitness, since the Bush School originated from the political science department and therefore appointing a liberal arts dean as an alternate represented a good fit.

The reasons for Dean Welsh's recusal are troubling. The GRC recognizes and appreciates the fact that Dean Welsh appears to be aware and genuinely concerned about the lack of diversity in the Bush School faculty, and outlined several steps and plans to overcome this deficit. However, it is troubling that as grounds for recusal, Dean Welsh characterized Dr. Bright as being aggressive, bullying, not civil, not respectful. This characterization stands in contrast to the DOF interactions with Dr. Bright. The DOF did indicate that Dr. Bright was a large individual, the implication being that his size could make him seem threatening. The GRC hopes that Dean Welsh and the DOF recognize that characterizing African American males as large, aggressive, and not respectful, evokes an awful and damaging Jim Crowe-era stereotype, a stereotype that should be assiduously shunned. Moreover, Dean Welsh and the DOF should attempt to see things from the perspective of the grievant. If you felt isolated and railroaded by the community, would you not be expected to engage in an aggressive and vigorous verbal defense?

Lack of Dean Welsh's recusal from the subsequent review of Dr. Bright's annual review (see below). It is curious that Dean Welsh did not continue to recuse himself from future oversight of Dr. Bright. Dean Welsh's recusal from the promotions review was an appropriate affirmation of an inability to be fair and impartial. According to the DOF, however, recusal on that basis cannot and should not be reversed. You cannot un-ring the bell. The GRC agrees with the DOF's verbalized position that it is inappropriate for Dean Welsh to have provided oversight over Dr. Bright's annual review.

Findings: The GRC finds that it was appropriate for Dean Welsh to recuse himself, though the underlying reasons for recusal are troubling. However, the recusal should be permanent. Perceptions of bias cannot be un-perceived.

Recommendations: In recusing himself, Dean Welsh behaved appropriately in this instance. However, the DOF needs to train deans and other administrators in implicit bias and the impact of words and perceptions on the success of minority faculty.

Overall Recommendations

The promotions process having been contaminated by the failure to recuse, and by other problems should be started anew and without prejudice. Every effort needs to be made to ensure that implicit bias is eliminated from promotions committees. Promotions committees should also balance the need to find excellence with faculty advocacy.

Concerns about discriminatory practices and other ancillary issues

There is a clear set of facts outlined by Dr. Bright, that is not disputed by either the respondents or the fact witnesses. For each event viewed in isolation, there is then a plausible case for denial of bias or animus. However, as the villain in the James Bond movie famously said, *"once is happenstance, twice is coincidence, the third time it's enemy action."* Therefore, the sum totality of events outlined in the grievances and supporting documentation, does give an outsider pause. Perhaps there is indeed a case to be made, if not for outright racial discrimination, then certainly for the pervasive presence of implicit bias and disparate impact. At the very least, Dr. Bright, the sole African American tenured faculty, appears to be isolated and according to the testimony of others who were interviewed, was not adequately advised, and mentored. Based on the evidence provided and the interviews, the overall reaction of the GRC was that his claim of discrimination seemed justified.

Appendix L

Overall, the atmosphere in the department was such that the GRC strongly felt that the work environment for Dr. Bright was unfriendly and hostile.

At the outset, there was a remarkable lack of racial empathy. All three members we interviewed emphasized the smallness of the department. Mr. Welsh, Drs. Ramsdel and Green mentioned that they take care of each other in the department. Given the emphasis on collegiality otherwise, the general lack of empathy or collegiality that all three members displayed against Dr. Bright signified that relationships were sufficiently strained such that Dr. Bright would construe the environment as hostile towards him.

For a public policy-focused department, diversity is an important criterion. The department members acknowledged that they struggle to become more diverse. Yet, the overwhelming feeling that the GRC got was that the department was not fully sensitive to racial issues. We also felt that the department did not go far enough to take steps to retain and recruit minorities. Interviewed department members appeared to be unaware of concepts like disparate impact or implicit bias. At least one department member wondered whether the GRC wanted them to apply lesser standards to minorities. This, to the GRC, reflected a lack of sensitivity to the realities that universities face in their efforts to recruit, mentor and retain highly qualified URM faculty.

Dr. Ramsdel specifically mentioned that a big part of the promotion process included asked others for an *"informal assessment"* of whether one is ready for promotion. It was clear that a faculty member in the department could not completely rely on the objective criteria for teaching, service, and research as being determinative of the promotion process. Yet, apparently, no one objectively guided and advised Dr. Bright not to apply for promotion, presumably because he was not ready. Given the lack of collegiality towards Dr. Bright, the fact that Dr. Ramsdel did not get along with him, the GRC felt that the *"informal assessment"* clearly hurt Dr. Bright as the sole tenured African American faculty member in the department who did not get the benefit of advice that someone else would have.

Recommendations for Dr. Bright

The GRC believes that the claims of inherent bias that Dr. Bright has raised seem justified under the circumstances. The GRC believes that Dr. Bright should be entitled to a fair review for promotion by following the guidelines of the department strictly and by ensuring that members solicited to write the report are impartial and at arms-length with each other as required by the guidelines

Recommendations for the Department/Bush School

1. All members of the department except Dr. Bright should be subject to mandatory and in-person diversity training
2. The department should be clearly instructed to do their best to hire racially diverse faculty for the next four to five hires.
3. The DOF should commission mediation, such that the air with Dr. Bright is cleared with all members of the department, such that there is mutual respect.
4. It will not be out of line to have someone talk with Dr. Bright to understand his frustrations, perhaps have him go through training as well to clear some air and have a mediator work with everyone in the department to clear the air. The DOF should perhaps take this up with some level of urgency.

General Recommendations for the Dean of Faculties

It is possible, even likely that I would think that some of the disputes brought before the University Grievance Committee will be further litigated in a court-of-law. For the DOF, it is imperative

Appendix L

to take remedial actions with some level of urgency, so that the University proactively deals with potential systemic deficiencies

1. The DOF should include a note on the guidelines regarding conflicts of interest. All employees at the DOF office should be informed in writing to provide all guidance on the subject only in writing.

2. DOF should conduct mandatory training for all deans, department heads, administrators on diversity, inherent bias, and tolerance to proactively avoid such issues in the future and as part of TAMU's diversity initiative.

3. The DOF should conduct workshops using DOF members in interested units on the true value of the University Grievance process and its purpose. This will help the departments actively resolve disputes internally and create a positive work environment and culture that serves to mitigate, as opposed to escalate grievances, the establishment and maintenance of practical as opposed to rhetorical application of the AGGIE Code and the AGGIE Core Values.

4. DOF should perhaps consider instructing all departments, schools, deans, and units with some urgency to do the following.

    - to be mindful of and identify their *"centers of power"* and ensure that there is both racial and gender diversity in these centers of power. Centers of power are typically department heads, associate deans and such other positions served by tenured faculty. Using evidence for gender diversity as an excuse to not include racial diversity exacerbates issues of race.

    - to take active efforts to recruit and retain diverse faculty not just at the units but also as part of centers of power and to recycle these positions at reasonable intervals of 3 to 4 years to prevent accumulation of power by a few people.

5. The DOF needs to specifically educate deans and other administrators on the disparate impact on diversity of not duly appointing diverse candidates in centers of power and rotating them periodically for those positions within reasonable timeframes of 3 to 4 years.

6. The DOF needs to consider adopting the revised SAP 12.99.99.M0.01 (as recommended by the Texas A&M University Grievance Committee) with some urgency.

INDEX

A

academia-land, 116
academic culture, 6
academic determination, 7, 110, 237
academic freedom, 6, 116
academic work culture, 1
academic workplaces, xii, 2, 138
administrative role, 45, 182
advocate, 15, 134, 154, 155, 245
Aggie Code, 106, 224
aggressive, 114
Air Force, 42, 102, 140, 144, 145, 151
allies, 79
alternative dean, 83, 85, 109
ambiguity, 9, 13, 124, 129, 135
American Association of University Professors (AAUP), 6, 7, 139
anger, 41, 85, 156
annual evaluation, 82, 83, 222
annual review, 77, 89, 90, 95, 214, 217, 218, 221, 223, 237, 241, 246
Appendix A, 15, 154
Appendix B, 37, 159
Appendix C, 47, 168
Appendix D, 48, 177
Appendix E, 50, 200
Appendix F, 69, 203
Appendix G, 79, 213
Appendix H, 88, 217
Appendix I, 107, 225
Appendix J, 108, 231
Appendix K, 113, 236
Appendix L, 115, 239
arm's length, 49, 122
assistant professors, 9
associate professor, 3, 4, 8, 10, 16, 33, 35, 36, 37, 38, 45, 71, 73, 94, 106, 155, 159, 161, 162, 163, 165, 177, 187, 189, 209, 211, 213, 217, 220, 236, 239, 241

B

Banks, Katherine University President, 31, 104, 112, 113
biases, 6, 83, 115
Black faculty, 10, 89, 113, 120, 223, 236, 237, 238, 244
Blame-Shifting Game, 98
Bright, Christina, 1, 21, 111
bully, 97, 99, 101, 114
Bush School of Government and Public Service, 4, 33, 187, 189
Bush, George H. W. U.S. President, 34
bylaws, 210, 213, 222, 224

C

categorical denial, 29

Index

character assassination, 102
cheating, 25, 84, 102, 145, 149, 220, 223, 241
Chronicle of Higher Education, 114, 120, 141, 144, 147, 148, 149
college professor, 1, 131
College Promotion Committee (CPC), 16, 17, 19, 20, 21, 28, 63, 64, 69, 70, 71, 77, 89, 90, 126, 159, 210, 212, 220
collegiality, 1, 17, 125, 126, 218, 248, 249
compelling reasons, 7, 31
complaints, 13, 19, 20, 22, 24, 81, 86, 87, 88, 96, 101, 110, 115, 124, 128, 220
confidence, 18, 20, 31, 60, 64, 127
conflict of interest, 23, 24, 49, 84, 97, 239, 241, 243, 245, 250
conformity, 3, 126
consensus, 36, 125
contaminated, 28, 242, 243, 245, 247
contamination, 19, 25, 70, 115
Crocker, Ryan Dean, 4, 37, 38, 40, 41, 42, 75, 155, 217

D

D.A.R.V.O, 85
Dean of Faculties (DOF), 18, 19, 20, 22, 23, 24, 25, 53, 83, 84, 87, 105, 114, 120, 141, 162, 221, 223, 239, 240, 241, 242, 243, 244, 245, 246, 247, 249, 250, 251
declaration of war, 86
deliberation letters, 28, 112
deliberation memos, 11, 27, 47, 69, 77, 134
department head, 4, 11, 15, 17, 18, 21, 22, 28, 29, 35, 38, 41, 42, 46, 47, 51, 63, 69, 70, 71, 75, 77, 81, 89, 90, 93, 98, 116, 137, 154, 203, 207, 210, 211, 213, 219, 236, 239, 240, 241
Department Promotion Committee (DPC), 15, 19, 21, 22, 36, 37, 39, 48, 51, 63, 64, 69, 70, 73, 75, 76, 77, 89, 90, 112, 161, 203, 207, 210, 211, 221, 243

disloyal, 3
disparate treatment, 90
disparities, 10, 22, 237
diversity, equity, and inclusion (DEI), 115
Diversity, Equity, and Inclusion (DEI), 115, 141
documents, xi, 11, 13, 27, 28, 47, 90, 115, 142, 159, 205, 239
dossier, 11, 35, 47, 48, 49, 69, 70, 83, 89, 140
double-stacking, 59, 60, 64
draft copy, 114
dumbfounding, 9

E

economist, 107, 227, 232
Equal Employment Opportunity Commission (EEOC), xi, 3, 4, 11, 13, 18, 23, 25, 26, 27, 28, 29, 33, 34, 42, 53, 65, 85, 96, 97, 98, 106, 111, 125, 133, 157, 220, 221, 236, 237
evaluation process, 49, 106, 119, 127, 134
external reviewers, 11, 14, 15, 28, 46, 47, 48, 49, 50, 51, 52, 53, 54, 60, 61, 62, 63, 65, 66, 67, 69, 76, 79, 91, 101, 112, 122, 123, 129, 134, 135, 136, 155, 164, 185, 205, 219, 221, 236, 245

F

fight for fairness, 12
final report, 105, 114, 115, 159, 160, 237
finalist, 104, 159
former co-workers, 102, 129, 221
full professor, 1, 8, 9, 10, 11, 15, 18, 22, 29, 30, 31, 37, 40, 45, 46, 51, 55, 56, 63, 65, 66, 69, 71, 73, 83, 85, 86, 90, 91, 95, 96, 100, 111, 113, 120, 124, 131, 139, 154, 157, 168, 178, 181, 185, 186, 189, 192,

194, 195, 203, 204, 205, 206, 207, 209, 210, 211, 212, 217, 219, 220, 223, 236, 237, 239, 241

G

general-field journals, 36, 75, 95, 112
Gerber, Professor, 73, 75, 77, 95, 155, 158
Gig 'em, 34
gloated, 123
gold standard, 8
Google Scholar, 72, 73, 74, 75, 112, 170, 178, 184, 191, 194, 211, 215
graduate school, 1, 45
Green, Susan Dr., 15, 16, 17, 18, 29, 30, 42, 60, 81, 82, 83, 89, 91, 106, 116, 154, 155, 156, 157, 158, 203, 219, 220, 221, 222, 236, 239, 241
grievance, 82, 87, 96, 98, 105, 111, 132, 166, 221, 223, 239, 240
guidelines, 49, 50, 51, 53, 58, 61, 64, 75, 76, 106, 115, 140, 142, 160, 163, 180, 210, 221, 223, 236, 243, 249, 250

H

Hannah-Jones, Nikole Dr., 127
H-index, 63, 73, 140
history of hostility, 102, 136
Hopkins, Dr., 4, 35, 37, 41, 42, 46, 93, 154, 156
hostile workplace, 3
human resource management, 258

I

improper communication, 53
independent, 48, 49, 67, 86, 105, 123, 127, 135, 151, 161, 164, 165, 177, 203, 210, 221, 236
insulation, 129
interview, xi, 34, 87, 113, 126, 160

J

Jim Crow-era stereotypes, 114
Johnson, Dr., 42, 46, 47

L

lawsuit, 42, 110, 125
legal loopholes, 110

M

master's-only degree program, 34, 63
McCoul, Melissa Dr., 116
McElroy, Kathleen Dr, 113, 127, 237, 238
military leaders, 103
mistreatment, 3, 41
multiple authors, 8
multistage evaluation processes, 5, 125

N

national academy members, 66
National Center for Educational Statistics, 10, 120
NCAA Southeastern Conference Schools, 120
neutrality, 123

O

Office of Risk, Ethics, and Compliance (OREC), 24, 25, 26, 27, 28, 29, 88, 126, 128, 133, 221
off-the-record, 236
opening statement, 88
outmaneuver, 137

P

peer-accredited schools, 66
performance, 2, 3, 4, 5, 6, 7, 8, 9, 11, 12, 16, 18, 28, 30, 34, 38, 45, 67, 77, 78, 79, 81, 91, 92, 95, 97, 101, 113, 119, 124, 125, 131, 134, 136, 138, 154, 157, 158, 162, 163, 165,

171, 188, 207, 210, 213, 214, 215, 218, 220, 236, 237
performance improvement plan, 82
personal animosity, 103
play itself out, 22, 134
plea to the jurisdiction, 110
political science, 34, 61, 215, 245
position statement, 26, 27, 28
proficiency exams, 103
promotion, 139, 140, 142
provost, 3, 22, 24, 25, 28, 29, 31, 35, 45, 84, 89, 105, 106, 109, 137, 142, 156, 168, 175, 180, 184, 206, 208, 213, 218, 221, 222, 237, 240, 241
public service motivation, 36, 71, 155, 165, 168, 177, 180, 181, 182, 187, 188, 190, 196, 197, 198, 204, 209, 211, 258
public testimony, 113

Q

qualifiers, 129

R

racial discrimination, 22, 25, 28, 115, 120, 247
Ramsdel, Dr., 17, 19, 20, 21, 22, 23, 24, 25, 29, 41, 46, 47, 51, 52, 53, 54, 55, 56, 57, 58, 59, 60, 61, 64, 75, 76, 88, 93, 112, 115, 116, 123, 155, 217, 219, 220, 221, 239, 240, 241, 242, 243, 244, 248
recusal, 82, 83, 84, 98, 115, 222, 241, 242, 244, 245, 246
research standards, 16, 95, 154, 157
resentment, 2, 4, 131
retaliation, 22, 25, 30, 84, 85, 101, 106, 109, 115, 128, 156, 217, 220, 223, 224, 236
Reviewer 1, 61, 67, 140, 177, 205
Reviewer 2, 54, 181
Reviewer 3, 57, 58, 140, 185
Reviewer 4, 55, 56, 59, 61, 187
Reviewer 5, 59, 60, 63, 76, 189

Reviewer 6, 59, 64, 140, 196, 205
rigged, 1, 105

S

silenced dissent, 17
single-authored, 8, 71, 73, 165, 204, 209
single-authored publications, 8
sitting ducks, 134
solicitation, 48, 49, 50, 60, 61, 67, 69, 70, 76, 122, 123, 136
sovereign immunity, 129
strategic, 51, 208
subjective performance goals, 6

T

TABLE 1, 62
TABLE 2, 72
TABLE 3, 74
TABLE 4, 78
TABLE 5, 121
tenure, xi, 1, 2, 3, 4, 5, 6, 7, 8, 9, 10, 12, 18, 28, 33, 35, 36, 37, 38, 39, 45, 49, 57, 62, 65, 67, 75, 77, 78, 79, 92, 94, 95, 113, 119, 120, 122, 124, 127, 129, 131, 133, 134, 135, 140, 142, 146, 155, 157, 159, 160, 161, 162, 163, 164, 166, 168, 171, 180, 185, 190, 209, 213, 239, 240, 241
tenure and promotion, 2, 33, 39, 50, 62, 113, 159, 162
tenure review, 3, 4, 28, 35, 67, 77, 79, 136, 164, 171, 185, 190, 241
Texas Scorecard, 115
The Bright Professor, xii, 139, 140

U

uncivil, 97, 99
unfit for public service, 97, 100, 114
United States President Obama's Administration, 42
University Grievance Committee (UGC), 86, 87, 88, 89, 90, 91, 92,

256

94, 95, 98, 99, 100, 101, 105, 106, 114, 115, 116, 119, 126, 140, 217, 221, 223, 224, 237, 249, 251
University of Georgia, 29, 49, 62, 64, 121, 134, 136, 142, 190
University of Louisville, 2, 3, 4, 11, 33, 34, 35, 36, 38, 40, 86, 120, 134, 136, 142, 157, 158, 161, 164, 167
University of South Alabama, 2, 33, 175
university president, 3, 31, 35, 69, 70, 75, 103, 112, 113, 116, 127, 135
unsubstantiated, 30, 128

V

Vaughn, Dr., 71, 73, 75, 95, 155, 158
voted, 4, 11, 15, 21, 31, 35, 36, 37, 70, 71, 112, 154, 203, 207, 212, 219

W

Washington Post, 114, 150
Welsh, Mark Dean and University President, 15, 16, 18, 20, 21, 22, 23, 24, 25, 42, 71, 82, 83, 84, 85, 89, 90, 91, 93, 94, 95, 97, 98, 99, 100, 101, 102, 103, 106, 109, 112, 113, 114, 115, 116, 120, 126, 137, 140, 151, 154, 218, 220, 221, 222, 223, 236, 237, 238, 239, 241, 245, 246, 247
wiggle room, 129
workplace survival strategies, 132

Y

Young, Michael Dr., 31, 86, 89, 104, 127
YouTube, xii, 88, 139, 140

ABOUT THE AUTHOR

Dr. Leonard Bright is a professor at Texas A&M University's Bush School of Government & Public Service. He earned his Ph.D. in Public Administration and Policy from Portland State University's Hatfield School of Government. His specialties are public service motivation, public management, human resource management, organizational behavior, and higher education. His research achievements are highly regarded and appear in leading publications within his field. He has held various leadership and academic positions at the national, state, and university levels. These included serving as the President of the Southeastern Conference for Public Administration (SECoPA), President of Metro Louisville's American Society of Public Administration (ASPA) Chapter, Vice President of the American Association of University Professors (AAUP) Texas Conference East Region, Assistant Provost in the Office of Graduate and Professional Studies and Assistant Dean of Graduate Education in the Bush School of Government and Public Service at Texas A&M. Currently, he is the President of the American Association of University Professors Chapter at Texas A&M University.

www.ingramcontent.com/pod-product-compliance
Lightning Source LLC
Chambersburg PA
CBHW070615030426
42337CB00020B/3812